THE
GREAT
AMERICAN
THINKERS
SERIES

This series of original works is designed to present in highly readable form the flow of American thought from colonial times to the present. Each volume has been written by a leading scholar and is devoted to a single man in the history of American thought who represents a particular trend or movement within the great span of our culture. Each book in the series contains a short biography of the man, a critical evaluation of his central ideas and their influence upon American thought as a whole, as well as an extensive bibliography and an index.

The Great American Thinkers Series is designed for the general reader as well as the serious college student or higher-level secondary school student, and is under the general editorship of two distinguished American educators: Arthur W. Brown, Dean of the Graduate School of Arts and Sciences and Professor of English, Fordham University, and Thomas S. Knight, Professor of Philosophy and Chairman of the Department of Philosophy, Adelphi College. *Henry David Thoreau* was written by James G. Murray, Professor of English and Chairman of the Department of English, Adelphi College.

☆

The GREAT AMERICAN THINKERS *Series*

JONATHAN EDWARDS • *Alfred Owen Aldridge*
BENJAMIN FRANKLIN • *Ralph L. Ketcham*
JOHN WOOLMAN • *Edwin H. Cady*
THOMAS JEFFERSON • *Stuart Gerry Brown*
JOHN C. CALHOUN • *Richard N. Current*
GEORGE BANCROFT • *Russel B. Nye*
CHAUNCEY WRIGHT • *Edward H. Madden*
CHARLES PEIRCE • *Thomas S. Knight*
WILLIAM JAMES • *Edward C. Moore*
THORSTEIN VEBLEN • *Douglas F. Dowd*
JOHN DEWEY • *Richard J. Bernstein*
ALEXANDER HAMILTON • *Stuart Gerry Brown*
JOSIAH ROYCE • *Thomas F. Powell*
GEORGE SANTAYANA • *Willard E. Arnett*
HENRY DAVID THOREAU • *James G. Murray*

IN PREPARATION

JAMES MADISON • *Neal Riemer*
RALPH WALDO EMERSON • *Warren Staebler*
THEODORE PARKER • *Arthur W. Brown*
ALFRED NORTH WHITEHEAD • *Nathaniel Lawrence*
DR. W. E. B. DU BOIS • *Henry Lee Moon*
NORMAN THOMAS • *Robert J. Alexander*

HENRY DAVID
THOREAU

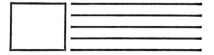

Author of this volume: James G. Murray, Ph.D., Professor and Chairman of the Department of English, Adelphi University.

Series Editors: Arthur W. Brown, Ph.D., Dean of the Graduate School, Fordham University; and Thomas S. Knight, Ph.D., Professor and Chairman of the Department of Philosophy, Adelphi University.

Twayne Publishers, Inc.   ::   New York

*This Twayne Publishers edition
is published by special arrangement with
Washington Square Press, Inc.*

"I am interested in an indistinct prospect, a distant view, a mere suggestion often, revealing an almost wholly new world to me. I rejoice to get, and am apt to present, a new view."

Journal (IX, 495):
July 29, 1857

FOREWORD

In keeping with the purposes of the Great American Thinkers series, and in accommodation of the unique qualities put forth by the subject, this study of Henry David Thoreau is not a life of the man but a biography of his mind. Indeed, to use his own term, it is a "meteorology" of that mind, a critical treatment of the (so to speak) physical laws informing its atmosphere and regulating its phenomena.

Since certain features of the treatment will be both immediately evident to the reader and persistent throughout the book, I think it prudent to explain what is going on here and why.

First, I employ primary sources almost exclusively. The reason is not that I distrust or mean to denigrate the many excellent approaches to Thoreau available to the general public in the form of biographies and to the scholarly professions in the form of specialized monographs and critical articles. It is, rather, that I believe the time has come for what might be called an original reading of this often analyzed, ultimately elusive man of letters, philosopher of the American consciousness, and moralist to the American conscience. What is needed, I am persuaded, is a presentation, out of his own work, of what he made of himself and what he wished his audience, then and now, to make of him.

Second, letting Thoreau speak for himself, I necessarily rely very heavily on quotations, seeing my essential task as the grouping of these quotations into meaningful patterns. Some interpretation is required, of course. In the main, however, I take it that my understanding of Thoreau is visible in the arrangement of the material even more than in my commentary on it.

Third, the Thoreau I know best and present here is most typically represented by his journals (which are as substantial to his total intellectual production as they are basic to this interpretation) and by his neglected fugitive pieces (which introduce different phases of his thought at the beginning of each chapter). This is not my way of saying that *Walden* or "Civil Disobedience" are overrated indexes to Thoreau as man or thinker. It is to say that we have become far too familiar with too few Thoreau texts for our own good. These are great items, surely. But their preparation and composition took up only a very small part of his career. We want to know what he thought before and after them. We want to know the steady whole of his intellectual life, not simply a few brilliant, possibly misleading parts of the whole.

Fourth, I deliberately emphasize those themes which recur most frequently in the Thoreau canon (high seriousness, individualism, idealism, his affinity for nature are examples) at the conscious risk of repetitiousness. What is more, my citations in illustration of these themes may sometimes seem removed from their original contexts. Both devices, as I see the matter, propose a single point: Although Thoreau lived long and variously, and although he addressed himself to many different kinds of topics in his published and unpublished works, he actually centered on only a very few concepts and formulated only a very few principles. To these he kept on returning, no matter what his subject of the moment. Repetition, moreover, is a characteristic of his thought. Insisting on this simply accords with his own insistence. As for the notion of context, I should say that the only real context is that identified by these few themes, to which all his topics tend. Therefore, for example, a citation drawn from a passage on religion but applied to a section on, let us say, nature or politics merely typifies his own studied practice and suggests the root simplicity of his thinking within the complexity of his interrelated interests.

Finally, if the tone of this book is observed to be moralistic, its expression exaggerated, and the shape of the whole, like the shape of each part, conforming to just one pattern (from the negative to the positive, from abuse to use, up the transcendental ladder from the most particular and grounded aspect of a subject to a most general, ideal, even mystical view of the same), again I submit that, in my view of Thoreau, these things are meant to be imitations. Thoreau was always and basically a moralist. As a naturalist he moralized. As a political economist he moralized. Ethics was really his only subject. On this subject he was given to preaching homilies. As a homilist, moreover, whether or not he had a congregation, he tended to overstate his lessons, not because he could not be reasonable or would not be cautious, but because the bland approach never reaches, much less touches and convinces, the timid. Having determined that, it remained for him to evangelize by a method that could be instantly recognized as his method: a setting forth of the right out of the wrong, of the ideal out of the real, of heaven out of hell.

On these patterns, then, not to borrow so much as to explicate, I have constructed and superimposed an overall structure. It is a way of reading Thoreau, a way of getting at the broad outlines of his intellectual history. It is not, obviously, the only way, nor does it pretend to be a search for or realization of Thoreauvian absolutes. (He was too large, too complex, and too contradictory a figure to subject to absolutes.) Nevertheless, this structure does provide a measurement of his dimension, an introduction to his way of thinking, and—hopefully—a chart of his thought.

Part I, called "Positioning," introduces the man and offers the manner and method of coming to know him. Fundamental to this knowledge is a grasp of his idea of the self and of his devotion to purpose in life.

Part II, called "Deflection," discusses those threats to the self, those impediments to purpose, which set a man back, which divert him from the one true goal. The chapters in this section are darkly negative—because there was, no doubt of it, a somber side of his nature and because, more importantly, he believed in the necessity of all men in the real life, as well as in their aspiration for the ideal, to realize and reckon with the several sorts of evil in the world before they can transcend them. In a word, this part maintains that Thoreau took some small steps backward before he assayed the giant step forward.

Part III, called "Conviction," is (as it were) the synthesis of "Positioning's" thesis and "Deflection's" antithesis. Even more, it presents to a basic man (Part I) who has been thoroughly chastened (Part II) the guide to the good life. His ground should be nature, his virtues simplicity and freedom, and his destiny and destination the kind of other world, or other-worldliness, to which pure thought should direct him.

Let it be understood that each of these parts represents Thoreau talking to himself. On the other hand, insofar as they put forth the only thought he put forth, they become his intellectual history *of* and moral message *to* the world.

☆

CONTENTS

PART I:

POSITIONING

Chapter 1

MEANING OF THE MESSAGE:
"MYTHOLOGICALLY IN EARNEST"

Great persons are not soon learned, not even their outlines, but they change like the mountains in the horizon as we ride along.[1]

My destiny is now arrived—is now arriving. I believe that what I call my circumstances will be a very true history of myself. . . . I welcome my fate for it is not trivial nor whimsical.[2]

In the summer of 1840, when he was young enough to seem brashly assertive and old enough to be confidently dogmatic, Henry David Thoreau composed a rather elaborately metaphorical and quite self-conscious essay called "The Service."[3] Taking his form from various peace and nonresistance pamphlets popular in New England at the time, he characteristically shaped the material to suit his own idiosyncratic purposes. These included the not unduly figurative notions that life was a war, that living was a type of military conscription, and that the soldierly recruit should possess certain qualities and conduct himself in prescribed ways.

Margaret Fuller, to whose *Dial* the finished piece was sent, kept it for half a year before rejecting it on the grounds that its argument was tortured, its thought did not flow, and its style was suggestive of the "grating of tools on the mosaic."[4] She could have added that the writing was paradoxical for the sake of paradox, much too metaphysically conceited, and deliberately, exasperatingly literary.

Read as a figure of speech, however, "The Service" is important in itself and for its implications. If nothing

[3]

else, it does two things: it points to Thoreau's more mature thought, and it indicates how he intended that thought to be understood. Indeed, it may be taken as a primer on his belief and a handbook of intepretation.

Most generally, the essay deals with bravery and fate, both of which terms (Thoreau notes) derive from the Latin root for fortitude and fortune *(fors)*, suggesting thereby a basic relationship between the quality of a man and the exigency of existence.

Thoreau sees bravery not so much "in resolute action as [in] healthy and assured rest." It is for him an inner attribute, not an external one, "having found a shorter way, through the observance of a higher art," to the essentials of being, with this art defined as nothing more nor less than the very "divinity in man," or "the true vestal fire of the temple." Would they but recognize the fact, all men, even the least conspicuous, possess in abundance "the materials of manhood" and, therefore, of bravery. The trouble is that most men are not "rightly disposed" to the recognition or the possession.

How to dispose them properly? First, by insisting that each have confidence in his own worth to the extent that he can say "I must wrap myself in my virtue" and mean what he says. Second, by demanding confidence in confidence itself, this to take the shape of an eager willingness to go it alone, without a sickly reliance on resources outside oneself. For nature, man's mother and prop, "refuses to sympathize with our sorrow; she has not provided for, but by a thousand contrivances, against it. . . ."

Bravery, then, is primarily being true to the self. What is fate? It is, simply, what will be. And, in the order of the universe as Thoreau appreciated that order, what will be is right: "Must it be so, then it is good." Putting this another way, Thoreau avowed that "to be necessary is to be needful, and necessity is only another name for inflexibility of good."

Another thing fate is, by way of martial similitude, is a strain of music heard as the "fixed measure" of the universe. But its sounds, one must realize, are not blatant; the soldier should march, not to what others hear, but to what he "thinks" he hears, ordering his whole life into "a stately march to an unheard music."

Moreover, Thoreau advises, fate is that which a particular man makes of a particular life, having little to do with the so-called will of the gods and nothing to do with the mores of the masses. It calls for singularity, "the testy spirit of knight errantry," "a steady progression" along the route of one's own decision, and the resolve that one must not be "defeated by the opportunities" of life but be their master.

In short, the recruit is summoned to be himself, his "service" viewed as nothing less than idealism. His pay or rewards will not be the usual ones—of money, medals, or honor in society's sense. Rather, such a recruit as Thoreau identifies must expect to be left "quite out of history," for this is the fate of the idealist, this "the life of a great man."

So speaking, Thoreau sounds very much like Tom Paine, another individualist and idealist, preaching integrity from a drumhead. The difference is that Paine's war was actual, Thoreau's symbolic; that Paine urged the worth of the cause over the worth of the self, whereas for Thoreau selfhood was the cause; and that Paine's idea of service was to redeem one's life by dying for one's country, as against the Thoreauvian precept of salvation through a life well lived. Both men marched to a battle, true. Thoreau's engagement, however, was mounted inwardly:

We are dreaming of what we are to do. Methinks I hear the clarion sound, and clang of corselet and buckler, from many a silent hamlet of the soul. The signal gun has long since sounded, and we are not yet on our posts. Let us make such haste as the morning, and such delay as the evening.[5]

Now it may be argued that "The Service," an early work with significance for later ones, was really an outline for a life yet to be lived. For the most part, furthermore, Thoreau did live that life as he had outlined it. Taken at face value only, the life (like the outline) lacks excitement and appears to lack importance. Metaphorically, both demand attention.

He was born on July 12, 1817, in Concord, Massachusetts, a small town as seething with revolutionary ideas as it was serenely sleepy to the eye. His family, tradition has it, was "different"—genteel, generous, serious-minded, hard to get along with, and provocative (particularly to the conservative and respectable). Thoreau took a Harvard degree in 1837, one of the few times he was separated from Concord and the family, but he was not impressed by that institution, the education it had provided, or the society it had fostered. Upon graduation, he taught for a time in the Concord school, and with his brother John in a school of his own founding and devising. Some lyceum lecturing, a brief stint at pencil making in the family business, and odd jobs as handyman and surveyor comprise his entire career as a wage earner. Of greater importance to him personally were the keeping of a journal (begun in 1837), a stimulating but ultimately disappointing association with Emerson and certain other neighboring Transcendentalists, semiprofessional (as writer or naturalist) excursions to Cape Cod, Maine, and Canada, and of course his two-year experiment in solitude and deliberate living on the shores of Walden Pond, not far from his own home.

In his lifetime he published two books only: *A Week on the Concord and Merrimack Rivers* (1849) and *Walden* (1854), both of which, deriving from meaningful, pleasure-filled experience, might have been his literary–philosophic way of making a mark upon the world, and neither of which earned him any money or gained him much attention. Although his formal career in letters and thought was sustained by an essay here, a poem there; and although he wrote (journal entries, letters, drafts of lectures) every day of his adult life, it can be fairly said that he was as much a professional land agent as he was a professional writer–thinker—if we are to judge by the demands his contemporaries placed upon either of his professions.

Twice in his life he came into public focus: when he

suffered a night in jail for refusing, out of conscience, to pay his taxes (reported in "Civil Disobedience," 1849); and when he goaded his complacent neighbors on the slavery issue (see "Slavery in Massachusetts," 1854, and "A Plea for John Brown," 1859). For the most part, however, he was content to be himself, to be by himself, discovering for himself the art of living. For the most part, too, society was content with his contentment.

Living interiorly (he paid attention to few and fewer still paid any attention to him) and heeding essentially only the sounds which emanated from "the silent hamlet of the soul," he made the most out of his life, lacking in excitement and importance as it seemed to be. "I do not the least care where I get my ideas, or what suggests them," he said;[6] but it is obvious that he derived a great deal from his reading, at least—in the Greek and Latin classics, the metaphysical poets of the seventeenth century and the Transcendentalists of the nineteenth, scientific treatises, travel literature, and various kinds of religious scriptures. He subscribed to no particular philosophy, and what was philosophical in him tended to be neither systematic nor consistent, yet he was able to discover transcendent thought patterns in routine observations of natural facts and everyday, commonplace living. He made his impact upon society without the platforms provided by school, church, state, or press. And he managed to solve his personal problems—how to have friends without encumbrances, the benefits of nature without sterile isolation, belief without institutionalized religion, and a busy, productive life without industry or industriousness—in the glorious challenges of daily existence, with considerable assistance from the two million probing words of his journal, which was to become his conscience and his consciousness.

Economical from his point of view (much from little), it was the kind of life which his contemporaries valued, if they valued it at all, ambivalently. The same Emerson, for example, who had complained that "Thoreau wants a little ambition in his nature. . . . Instead of being the head of American engineers, he is captain of a huckleberry party,"[7] praised him for his "simplicity and clear perception," and for making merry with this "double-dealing, quacking world."[8] However, it was Emerson who captured the spirit of Thoreau better than any—in his time or ours:

> He was a protestant *à outrance,* and few lives contain so many renunciations. He was bred to no profession; he never married; he lived alone; he never went to church; he never voted; he refused to pay a tax to the State; he ate no flesh, he drank no wine, he never knew the use of tobacco; and, though a naturalist, he used neither trap nor gun . . . bachelor of thought and nature . . . attorney of indigenous plants.[9]

The austerity of Thoreau's character and habits repelled some ("I love Henry, but I cannot like him; and as for taking his arm, I should as soon think of taking the arm of an elm-tree").[10] His apparent idleness disturbed others ("Think of it! He stood half an hour today to hear the frogs croak, and he wouldn't read the life of Chalmers!").[11] Some few at least could attest to the man's substance (Alcott said that if you were to get wine from a visit to Emerson, you would get venison from a talk with Thoreau),[12] whereas one, the redoubtable Channing, realized the nature of the demon which drove his friend Henry: "I see nothing for you in this earth but that field . . . ; go out upon that, build yourself a hut, and there begin the grand process of devouring yourself alive."[13]

Well, he did go into the field—to find himself, not to devour himself. What he found there differs considerably from what his neighbors thought of him and his life. What he said he found there provides the clue to what we might think.

Thoreau knew, and so advised us, that there was something of the unusual in him, explaining that something—with both honesty and modesty—in terms of genius. No one, he cautioned, could presume to advise a genius or pass judgment upon one, by which he meant that each man had a genius rather than that he himself was a genius in the common parlance. The reason is that only a genius "knows what he is aiming at; nobody else knows. And he alone knows when something comes between him and his object."[14] As he understood his own genius, it seemed to require two things of him: that he focus on what he called "the main chance," without regard to appearances and manners;[15] and that, however others might find his manner of living defective in contrast with theirs, he should keep looking ahead and beyond, without a special or undue concern for immediate consequences. As he put the matter, "I am interested in an indistinct prospect, a distant view, a mere suggestion often, revealing an almost wholly new world to me. I rejoice to get, and am apt to present, a new view."[16]

Such a view, of himself and of his world, was of course ideal, but it was not an ideal which contradicted reality. Rather it was a "reality . . . transcendentally treated"[17] that mattered to him. The phrase is essential to an understanding of Thoreau as a man and a thinker. There is a *reality* to him and his opinion, he thought, not simply an idle, perverse idea; but it must be regarded transcendentally, which is to say that, although it derives from ordinary and earthly experience, it climbs to the regions of the extraordinary and the pure. He was the first to realize and to confess his faults in the way that a simple, nontranscendental notion of reality would declare them. But he suggested that, transcendentally treated, even his faults and failings take on a significance we dare not miss. For example, he admitted that "my actual life is unspeakably mean, compared with what I know and see that it might be. Yet the ground from which I see and say this is some part of it. It ranges from heaven to earth and is all things in an hour."[18] As for his mission in life, the call of his particular genius, again he confessed that "I have felt mean enough when asked how I was to act on society, what errand I had to mankind. Undoubtedly I did not feel mean without a reason, and yet my loitering is not without defense."[19] Thus he saw himself, in a real context transcendentally interpreted, as an aristocratic guru whose function was to contemplate and to teach, not to act as other men do.

This function in part he would perform by his writing. In it, especially in the journal, he would describe how "the actual hero," not the imaginary one, "lived from day to day," not how a mistakenly moral, or moralistic, society dictated that he should live.[20] He would record the "joy and ecstasy" that daily living holds out to a man, at the same time warning himself—and us—that "in thy journal let there never be a jest! To the earnest there is nothing ludicrous."[21] Nor would he trouble himself—or any reader today—about the supposed distinction between recording facts and composing poetry, for "the most interesting and beautiful facts are so much the more poetry, and that is their success."[22]

Much as he liked to read and write, however, he seemed vaguely embarrassed about discharging his duty to his genius in a purely literary career. We find him questioning the reality of books and the sincerity of authors. Moreover, anyone living in Concord would have had some experience with bookish dilettantes. Writing must be incidental with him, therefore. His function would be living. "Ye fools," he cried out, "the theme is nothing, the life is everything."[23] His counsel to would-be readers, that "the real facts of a poet's life would be of more value to us than any work of his art,"[24] takes on a personally poignant meaning to a would-be writer (such as himself) when counterbalanced by this remark: "How vain it is to sit down to write when you have not stood up to live!"[25]

It was more important to him, then, that he live than that he write. By the same token, it is important that we see in his work the art of living rather than the act of writing. Not that he would "have any one adopt my mode of living on any account. . . . I desire that there may be as many different persons in the world as possible."[26] Nevertheless, there was and is a certain type of person who could profit from the art of his life as put forth in the life of his art: "the mass of men who are discon-

tented" with their own lives, perhaps because they have
paid too much attention to art, too little to life. Strong
and valiant natures, he felt, do not need his message,
neither do those "who find their encouragement and inspiration in precisely the present condition of things." But
that "most terribly impoverished class of all, who have
accumulated dross, but know not how to use it, or get
rid of it, and thus have forged their own golden or silver
fetters" do need the *exemplum* which his art makes out
of his life. To these he would be a local consciousness—
without prejudice to the possibility of serving also as a
national conscience. To such as these his life, or the
straight reporting thereof, its reality transcendentally observed, would say "something about your condition, especially your outward condition or circumstances in this
world, in this town, what it is, whether it is necessary that
it be as bad as it is, whether it cannot be improved as well
as not."[27]

Thoreau aimed to show his discontented fellow-Amer-
icans where they had gone wrong. Supposedly, they were
gregarious; his life extolled the virtue of a forgotten solitude. They were fact-prone; he would elucidate the poetic possibilities of fact. They were religious; he would
propose the notion of religion without church establishment. They were busy and industrious; he would demonstrate the efficacy of loitering. They thought they were
rugged individualists; detecting that they had little sense
of the self, he would put them on the path to self-dis-
covery.

The idea of success counted heavily with Americans.
Thoreau's life suggested a paradox (not merely a literary device, but much more of a religious symbol) to
them: the value of failure, at least in the sense that to
live one must first die. To those who saw success only in
terms of vocation he would spell out the larger vocation
of living, for which jobs and professions left no time. To
those sons and daughters of pioneers who had settled
down much too rapidly, preferring security to adventure,
community to individualism, and mediocrity to genius,
he would show what they had given up by disclosing the

delights of the road not taken. To those inheritors of political liberty who had left the promise of America unfulfilled he would show that, if personal liberty remains circumscribed by tradition and convention, political liberty not only counts for little but explains why that promise is unfulfilled. They had relied on law for liberty. They should have relied on life.

His neighbors in Concord could do with some instruction, too. Apparently they had accepted Transcendentalism (although Thoreau had some doubts about the turn it had taken in Concord), but even here, in this shrine of the other-worldly, there was too much talk of practicality. Thoreau's task would be to explain and to exemplify reality to realists, practicality to pragmatists. For it is neither real nor practical, he believed, to go on living "the mean life that we do." He would teach them that, for all their common sense, they would sicken and die because their "vision does not penetrate the surface of things."[28]

Having in fact penetrated this surface, Thoreau was in a position to see and say the real possibilities of contentment. Old patterns of life, those chiefly established in the East, were no longer satisfying. And so he turned to the Western frontier: "This is the only America I know. I prize this western reserve chiefly for its intellectual value. This is the road to new life and freedom."[29] But the point of this message, which is the meaning of Thoreau's life, is misread if we see it in terms of a campsite in the Rockies, a ranch in Montana, or a hut on Walden Pond. This reality transcendentally treated is actually a frontier of the spirit, something geographically inward and upward rather than literally westward. It is a practical reality he holds out for us—but it must be interpreted spiritually.

It might be asserted that, not having made a success of his life, Thoreau turned to the cold comfort of a diary, to the vicarious living of wishful thinking; that because his youth and vitality were slipping away without the fulfillment of one or the recognition of the latter, he lived by the artificial stimulation of remembrance rather than actually and really; and that his private writings, which came about because his public utterances were not accepted, merely amount to projections of what-might-have-been or sour-grapes expressions of what-had-been. Those who argue thus see a partial reality in Thoreau. What is worse, they see it too literally, not metaphysically enough. One can well imagine that the journal entries do indeed treat of his disappointment in love, his disenchantment with friends, his loneliness as well as his aloneness, his dejection devolving from rejection, and his real and anticipated encounters with sickness and death. These were his experiences, no question about that, and so he recorded them. But they are not to be read merely as facts. From them he learned, and what he learned he passed on. It isn't that, not being successful, he preached against success; or that, not being loved, he would recognize only an impossibly ideal love or none at all; or that, lacking friends, he turned to solitude and a justification of solitude; or that, unable to make his way in the commercial world, he turned, defensively, to nature. Rather each of these experiences teaches a lesson—transcendentally, metaphorically, mythologically. If so, then his legacy is instruction not in how to retreat from reality but how, as he did, to get the most from it.

Thoreau was quite insistent that we learn how to read the lessons of experience, and the manner in which he urges his own way suggests our way. He tells us that "it is only when we forget all our learning that we begin to know. . . . You must be aware that *no thing* is what you have taken it to be."[30] Indeed, it would seem that "some must work in fields if only for the sake of tropes and expression, to serve a parable-maker one day."[31] And again, all history (whether of the events of men or of the private experiences of a man) "put to a terrestrial use is mere history; but put to a celestial [or at least a metaphorical] is mythology always."[32]

As he understood the term, anyplace can be the source of mythology, even one's own neighborhood. This is because "the characteristics and pursuits of various ages and races of men are always existing in epitome in every neighborhood."[33] We may be charmed by distant prospects—"because we instantly and inevitably imagine a life to be lived there such as is not lived elsewhere"[34] —but "where we are," if not taken too literally, is source enough for the most distant prospects. Moreover, anything in any place can provide us, as the natural world did for Thoreau, with meanings both simple and marvelously mysterious: "These migrating sparrows all bear messages that concern my life. . . . I love the birds and the beasts because they are mythologically in earnest."[35]

Metaphorical speech, the kind which ultimately flowers into an earnest mythology of fact, is of necessity exaggerated. But it is not thus to be shunned, thought Thoreau. After all, he said, "We live by exaggeration. What else is it to anticipate more than we enjoy? The lightning is an exaggeration of the light. Exaggerated history is poetry. . . ."[36] In fact, he feared that his speech might not be extravagant enough, desiring "to speak somewhere without bounds,"[37] even if this "tempts me to certain licenses of speech." He stated precisely why he yielded to the temptation: because he had not his companion's (for this read the modern student of Thoreau) "sympathy in my sober and constant view. He asks for a paradox, an eccentric statement, and too often I give it to him."[38] In other words, because his companions (or we) fail to understand him when he speaks straightforwardly, he resorts to the indirections of trope, the suggestiveness of parable, the illuminating but sometimes illogical fancy of metaphor, and the grand design of myth. Understand, however, that such speech is not at odds with nature— nature itself, his nature, or the nature of his audience. It is of its essence.

Two examples, both oddly enough referring to the same geographical source, will explain his characteristic approach to metaphorical, earnestly mythological speech. In the first one, which comes at the end of a series of journal entries dealing with Thoreau's occasionally necessitated business ventures, he remarks on his return to solitude (simple loitering, if you will) and gives thanks as follows:

> It is the first silence I have heard for a month. My life had been a River Platte, tinkling over its sands but useless for all great navigations, but now it suddenly became a fathomless ocean. It shelved off to unimaginable depths.[39]

The second quote summarizes a general series of comments on the differences between existential and essential realities, or between what things (or persons) really are as against their superficial appearances:

> If the outside of a man is so variegated and extensive, what must the inside be? You are high up the Platte river, traversing deserts, plains covered with salt, with no deeper hollow than a prairie dog hole tenanted also by owls and venomous snakes.[40]

Both passages refer to Thoreau's experience, something he had undergone or observed. Each may be taken purely autobiographically; that is, as having no significance to anyone but Thoreau. Conceivably, too, each may be read as an exaggeration hurled, as it were, against the wind. But there is another way in which the modern reader may receive them: as metaphorical assertions that the real life of a man is interiorly deep, not superficially shallow; that within his depths are to be found both essential usefulness and true fulfillment, whereas his surface holds out only moral shallowness, meanness, and discontent. The River Platte, in its heights and depths, thus becomes a subject for mythology, particularly for him who is "mythologically in earnest."

This mythology, as often as not in the Thoreau canon, springs from or is to be located in a natural object, and is to be used as a guide to a natural philosophy. However, we should also be aware that Thoreau had a special manner of insinuating spiritual, even specifically religious, principles into this natural philosophy. That is, many of his suggestions for the living of the good life, while apparently *sui generis* readings of sermons from stones, may be traced to paraphrases of the Bible. Two examples will make the point clear:

Love is the wind, the tide, the waves, the sunshine. Its power is incalculable; it is many horse-power. It never ceases, it never slacks; it can move the globe without a resting place; it can warm without fire; it can feed without meat; it can clothe without garments; it can shelter without roof; it can make a paradise within which will dispense with a paradise without.[41]

To what end do I lead a simple life, at all, pray? That I may teach others to simplify their lives?— and so all our lives be simplified merely like an algebraic formula? Or not, rather, that I may make use of the ground I have cleared, to live more worthily and profitably? . . . As a preacher, I should be prompted to tell men, not so much how to get their wheat bread cheap, as of the bread of life compared with which that is bran. Let a man only taste these loaves and he becomes a skillful economist at once.[42]

The first passage compares favorably with St. Paul's famous doctrine on love (1 *Corinthians,* 13), while the second bears marked resemblance to several Johannine citations (for example, 4:7 ff. and 6:35 ff.). Both, like their scriptural counterparts, read spiritual messages into the commonplaces of a real existence. As Thoreau used them, however, they are parables for living directed to an audience in need of saving truths but unlikely, in a century of science and liberalism, to find them in the usual sources. If he can turn a flight of sparrows into a mythology, he can also rework standard religious texts so that they may be acceptable to those who would as quickly reject the spiritual life as the natural life. He spoke in figures—not for the sake of verbal play but for the higher disclosures of a life beyond the senses. Thus did he treat reality rather transcendentally and thus can he be regarded as "mythologically in earnest."

On the whole, then, Thoreau was satisfied with his life —not because his senses continually gratified him but because through the senses he had discovered something, an ideal something, to which the senses pointed. It was this something which made his life a success, the singular dimensions of which he would communicate to his fellows in confidence rather than in dejection. He seems to deal mainly with the kinds of objects which the senses can grasp, but it was his strategy to arrange and interpret these objects so as to reveal the mythology for which they stand. He felt that he had touched the bottom of life, and yet he could also "taste a spring cranberry, save a floating railing, feel the element fluctuate beneath me, and [be] tossed bodily as I am in thought and sentiment. Then longen folk to gon on voyages."[43] What he would have us see is not cranberries and railings but the mythical life they proposed.

Thoreau felt that he could guide "the folk" because he understood, as they did not, what they really needed: "All men want, not something to *do with,* but something to *do,* or rather something to *be.*"[44] He would teach them out of his own doings, metaphorically, tropically, mythologically, the possibilities of being. Out of his own rather small and (some said) mean existence he would put forth the hope for fulfillment, the spiritual attractiveness of which he found summarized in a passage from John Gower's poetry: "Thynke for to touche also / The world which neweth everie daie / So as I can, so as I maie."[45]

To "touche" this world, as one can and as one may, the writings of Thoreau suggest a certain program or schema (which is the order of the chapters which follow). One starts with a proper notion of the self because this is, or must be, the beginning of all other knowledge both natural and moral (Chapter 2). Then one ought to develop and maintain a sense of purpose so that meaning may be identified, direction established (Chapter 3). To know who one is and where he is going will not result in an instant paradise; at the very least, however, such knowledge will help him through a necessary confrontation with three obstacles to contentment: the tendency of the individual to undermine his own happiness (Chapter 4); the tendency of society, seen as friends or state, to misdirect the ends of this happiness (Chapter 5); and the tendency of a primal, innate evil, deep within the natures of both men and things, to blot out the sun (Chapter 6). Certain, now, because the tests have been passed, we move on to a meditation on nature, for this is the source of all earnest mythology (Chapter 7); to a consideration of those virtues, freedom and simplicity, which ensure entrance into the gates of heaven, whether earthly or ideal (Chapter 8); and, finally, to a consideration of heaven itself—heaven as aspiration, as character, as the infinitely mystical (Chapter 9).

Self comes first. Just as Emerson had divided the world into the me and the not-me, so also does Thoreau, with perhaps the difference that the former discovered the self through the world, whereas the latter discovered the world through the self.

It is a good starting point, because it is at hand, and mythologies are always near:

Think of the consummate folly of attempting to go away from *here*. . . . Here is all that you love, all that you expect, all that you are. Here is your bride-elect. . . . Here is all the best and all the worst you can imagine. What more do you want?[46]

Chapter 2

SENSE OF THE SELF:
"ANOTHER FURROW THAN YOU SEE"

You will find at Trollhate excellent bread, meat, and
wine—provided you bring them with you.[1]

How alone must our life be lived! We dwell on the
seashore, and none between us and the sea. . . .
None are traveling one road so far as myself.[2]

As were Romantics in general and Transcendentalists in
particular, Thoreau was very conscious of the self, which
is not the same thing as being self-conscious. For them
and him, mirror-gazing, far from an embarrassing pre-
occupation with the grace of one's own image, signified
the beginning of the search for knowledge—of the world,
of humankind, and even of divinity. The self was the first
principle of this knowledge, the key to it, or else there
was no key. Therefore, to start with and from the self
had to be considered an intuitively sound, if not logically
demonstrable, initial step toward more objective discov-
eries.

The fact is, however, that the self, ultimately trust-
worthy, needed immediate confirmations, the kind that
could be had from established selves. Thus the Romantics
were hero-worshipers as well as individualists. The Transcendentalists, those self-reliant ones, set themselves up
against the model of certain saints, or simply emulated
each other. And Thoreau, although usually wary of find-
ing his own eggs in another's basket, did from time to
time identify those tried selves whom he could admire
and imitate. These included, not at all strangely for Thoreau, the sages of antiquity, an Oriental mystic, a fellow
Concordian or two—and a Maine woodsman named

[19]

Joe Polis. Each had had something to give him, a contribution to make toward the understanding or formation of the inimitably Thoreauvian self.

But he praised no man more than, very curiously, Sir Walter Raleigh, nor did he ever discover as much about himself—what he was, what he would like to be, what the possibilities for fulfilled, committed selfhood could be —than he said he discovered in this sixteenth-century courtier, warrior, and explorer, superficially as unlikely a candidate for Thoreau's self-concern as might be imagined.

His journal entries and reading lists show that he had been studying Raleigh's *History of the World* in 1842–1843. What came out of this consideration was an extended biographical–critical piece, originally intended for *The Dial* Magazine (which folded in 1844 before it could carry the essay, if indeed it would) and not published until long after Thoreau's death. A very instructive monograph on Raleigh, the article tells us much about Thoreau.[3]

He saw Raleigh, to begin with, as a type of "heroic character," at the same time admitting that Raleigh's virtues, having a "grace and loftiness" to them, were not "distinctively great." Among savages he would have been chief (to Thoreau this is not, as it may seem, damning with faint praise). Among civilized people, he stood out not because he had a profounder or grander nature but—significantly—because he had "more nature" than other men. He was enthusiastic. Good, says Thoreau. Extravagant. Good again. He had a presence which bespoke a confident, well-founded pride. "A proper knight, a born cavalier," he was his own man, one who "took counsel with the winds only" and not with the Queen or her fawning court. Praise him, Thoreau exclaims, for there are not many like him.

Understandably, Thoreau played down Raleigh's career as fighter and statesman, played up the man as explorer, poet, and martyr. Raleigh dared to invade, to confront, the unknown. He dared, indeed, to know. As an explorer, he met Thoreau's standards of the scientist:

[20]

a simple, natural observer. Thoreau could appreciate Raleigh's appreciation of what other men might reject as savage, quoting Raleigh's praise of Guiana with relish: "a country never sacked, turned, nor wrought; the face of the earth hath not been torn, nor the virtue and salt of the soil spent by manurance."[4] It was also important to Thoreau that it was not the desire for sudden and cheap wealth which brought Raleigh to the wilderness but the "splendor of the enterprise itself."

Raleigh the writer impressed Thoreau for three reasons: although "his philosophy is for the most part poor, yet the conception and expression are rich and generous"; he wrote his poems "rather with ships and fleets and regiments of men and horses," giving thereby the "warranty of life and experience" instead of the smell of the library; and his "perfectly healthy" sentences express the sturdy, "standard English" of the sturdy, standard Englishman.

As for Raleigh's martyrdom, Thoreau suggests that his death not only crowned his life but was a commendation of it. A many-talented man, he was not permitted by a jealous world to live to the happy old age which his interests and enthusiasms reserved for him. He was misunderstood, and so had to fall back on basic virtues which could not save his life but which did glorify his death: honesty, nobility, gentleness. Thoreau thought Raleigh's final utterances quite splendid, in themselves and in their reflection of these virtues. "It would be an unspeakable advantage," he quotes Raleigh, "both to the public and private, if men would consider that great truth, that no man is wise or safe but that he is honest. All I have designed is peace to my country; and may England enjoy that blessing when I shall have no more proportion in it than what my ashes make."[5] Again, the brave, sincere words from the gibbet—"It mattered little how the head lay, provided the heart was right"—attested at the moment of death to the fundamental morality of the self which had, in the prime of life, expressed itself in a "noble nature and gentle heart."

Thoreau's treatment of Raleigh seems much more an

apology than a scholarly analysis. It reveals that Raleigh had the faults of a soldier and courtier, that he was not quite original or independent, and that "withal his aspirations he was ambitious." Moreover, it indicates a typically Thoreauvian criticism of even the best of men: "What he touches he adorns by a greater humanity and native nobleness, *but he touches not the truest nor deepest.*" Still, all in all, Thoreau's Raleigh is put forth defensively, as if brother would protect brother, self stand for kindred self. Raleigh is not a perfect model for Thoreau's self (there can be no such), but for a young, romantic idealist he will do.

In fact, the utility of such a model is Thoreau's final point. Raleigh's life suggests "that a man is not to be measured by the virtue of his described actions, or the wisdom of his expressed thought merely, but by that free character he is, and is felt to be, under all circumstances."[6] In other words, what Raleigh was, not what he did, commends him. What we should "read" is his self, not his biography. The self, quite apart from the biography, teaches us "not to despair of the race"; the bravery of that self, by contrast, teaches us that "heroism today is dyspeptic"; and that self's capacity for vigor and enthusiasm teaches us that "gross health and cheerfulness are no slight attraction," particularly for an anemic, cloistered society.

We can learn, then, from "this fair specimen of an Englishman in the sixteenth century." But the essential lesson is that "it behooves us to be fairer specimens of American men in the nineteenth," not carbon copies. The message is twofold: that each man should choose the right model for selfhood, not the expected one; and that each, for all the influence of the model, should be his own man. To this message can be added a corollary: what Thoreau made out of Raleigh can be made out of Thoreau. In putting forth Raleigh's self, he effectively displayed his own.

Thoreau gave two explanations for talking about himself as much as he did. One, it is the subject he knew best: "I should not talk so much about myself if there were any body else whom I knew as well. Unfortunately, I am confined to this theme by the narrowness of my experience."[7] The other proposes a higher, or at least less egotistical, purpose: "If I seem to boast more than is becoming, my excuse is that I brag for humanity rather than for myself."[8] The first explanation tells the reader that knowledge of the self is limited but not necessarily delimiting. The second says that, given the communal nature of humanity, one self properly understood illumines all selves. With Thoreau, as with Socrates, to know thyself is fundamental to both life and thought.

What did he think of himself? Somewhat perversely, Thoreau admitted to and even took pride in his low estate. "I regard myself as a good deal of a scamp,"[9] he said, suggesting also that there was "some advantage in being the humblest, cheapest, least dignified man in the village, so that the very stable boys shall damn you."[10] Although one may think of these comments as a form of inverse snobbery, it is more likely that they were—and should be taken as—basic realism. At any rate, Thoreau would feel, they are a better (that is, more honest) starting point for self-knowledge than would be some form of personal exaltation or social complacency.

In the same vein, he could say that "brown is the color for me, the color of our coats and our daily lives, the color of the poor man's loaf"[11] and mean something morally fundamental for humanity, not just something personally denigrating. Or he could say that "the sight of a marsh hawk in Concord meadows is worth more to me than the entry of the allies into Paris. In this sense I am not ambitious."[12] Again, the meaning would not be something deprecatory or churlish, but something positive and worthy of imitation in the sense that the self described chose a higher value over a lesser one.

To know the self is to see it fundamentally, to realize its elemental properties. Then one can go on, as Thoreau did, to the loftier reaches. "I know of no redeeming qualities in me but a sincere love for some things. . . . Therein I am God-propped,"[13] he asserted. From things to divinity, or at least to the fulfillment of divine purposes, is the progression of the self. Moreover, while trying to *be* at the expense of trying only to *do,* the self can make virtues out of what society would call vices: "In idleness I am of no thickness. I am thinnest wafer. I never compass my own ends. God schemes for me."[14] Such is a fair price to pay for "loafing."

A lordly god may always be discovered within the lowliest of loafing selves. In this sense God does not war with the self. It does have other enemies, however. One is a society which does not understand in us that unique quality (selfness itself?) which makes "us poor neighbors and friends." This is so because it would treat of and deal with externals, whereas selfness is something more difficult to discern: "However intense my experience, I am conscious of the presence and criticism of a part of me which, as it were, is not a part of me, but spectator, sharing no experience, but taking note of it."[15] Whereas Thoreau would occasionally blame this lack of communication, this critical isolation, on himself ("But I do not melt; there is no thaw in me; I am bound out still"[16]), more often the failure to penetrate and thus be able to communicate, much less have the right to criticize, is that of society, not of the self.

Another foe to the realized self is the unrealizing self, that which falls below expectations and potentials. The drive of the self is "to make my life a sacrament. What is nature without this lofty tumbling? May I treat myself with more and more respect and tenderness. May I not forget that I am impure and vicious."[17] Or, as he wrote to a friend who would meet him rather than read his books:

You may rely on it that you have the best of me in my books, and that I am not worth seeing personally —the stuttering, blundering, clod-hopper that I am. Even poetry, you know, is in one sense an infinite brag and exaggeration. Not that I do not stand on all that I have written—but what am I to the truth I feebly utter?[18]

[24]

The self-criticism in these passages, it will be noted, is not based primarily on external grounds (that he stutters or blunders), and is not deserved because he has not tried to put forth the best that was in him. The real fault was that he himself, in his inner self, always seemed to be so much less than its mission demanded of it, or of the expectations he had for it.

Nevertheless, whatever he might be was predicated on what he was. The best that he was took cognizance of the worst. Indeed, the sense of his own meanness, one of the central themes in his journal, is so strong, so convincing, that we tend to see it as an advanced case of self-doubt and guilt. But it is more than that. It suggested to Thoreau how much better he might be. To his readers it should suggest not the probability of despair but the possibility of spiritual revival. For out of faults, however demeaning, are virtues perfected.

Thoreau was critical of himself in specific terms and for particular reasons. First, he tended to accuse himself of not demanding more of himself. At one point in his life, he worded the fault this way: "I exact less of myself. I am getting used to my meanness, getting to accept my low estate. . . . If I could feel anguish at each descent!"[19] At another the trouble seemed to be that "I have grown more coarse and indifferent."[20] Second, he would blame himself for every instance of falling below standards that he would set for others, this in the manner of the saint who had sunk to the level of the sinner. For example, he was scornful of those who sought their wealth in gold (more specifically, in gold-digging) because they lived by luck and not by vision. And yet, thinking over "my own unsatisfactory life, doing as others do," he judges himself guilty of conducting his life "without any fixed star habitually in my eye, my foot not planted on any blessed isle."[21] Or he would preach the gospel of nature only to go "through the process of killing the cistudo for the sake of science—but I cannot excuse myself for the murder"[22] or taking part in an animal hunt which he describes as "this afternoon's tragedy" because it "affected the innocence" of his errand into the blessed wilderness and proved him to be as "base or coarse" as any other sportsman.[23] Third, he frequently upbraided himself for insensibility (in the root meaning of the term) as he did for insensitivity. "Will wonder become extinct in me?" he questioned; "Shall I become insensible as a fungus?"[24] As he matured, would he lose the freshness of instinct, the enthusiasm of immediate response? Would intellect crowd out sensation?—"My life was ecstasy . . . before I lost any of my senses."[25] In short, would he grow up to adult meanness, away from youthful innocence, and thus repeat the fall from paradise —despite the fact that his self knew better?

Meanness degrades a man. This is his point, not simply that he has been mean. A self that is less than it ought to be, moreover, is *naturally* as well as *morally* wrong. Such a self would "make a huge effort to expose my innermost and richest wares" but succeed only in exhibiting a "counter . . . cluttered with the meanest home-made stuffs."[26] Such a self thwarts the purposes of nature, of life itself, because "the thought of what I am, of my pitiful conduct, deters me from receiving what joy I might from the glorious days that visit me."[27] Such a self delimits life's possibilities in a most frustrating way. For—

> Each more melodious note I hear
> Brings this reproach to me
> That I alone afford the ear
> Who would the music be.[28]

But if Thoreau explicitly warns against the dangers to selfhood, suggesting by an honest analysis and painful criticism of these dangers the need to reject the false self, he is equally explicit, as far as his own nature was concerned, about the way (the word is used in the Taoist sense) to the true self.

Surely the first step is not only a recognition of but an emphasis on the individuating quality of the individual, the independent selfness of the self. He tells us, urgently it would seem, that "we are constantly invited to be what we are; as to something worthy and noble. I never waited but for myself to come 'round; none ever detained me, but I lagged or tagged after myself."[29] This independence of self frees a man "from public opinion, from government, from religion, from education, from society."[30] It is the complement of "a manly sincerity." Possessing it, "you shall not be trifled with but drive this business of life. It matters not how many men are to be addressed, rebuked—provided one man rebuke them."[31] There are risks to it, to be sure, not the least of which is that independence of self may seem to render a man, by society's standards, characterless: "The greatest impression of character is made by that person who consents to have no character. He who sympathizes with and runs through the whole circle of attributes cannot afford to be an individual."[32] But the game is infinitely worth the candle, because independence of the self is self-fulfilling, is (one might say) its own reward and excuse for being: "Thus much at least a man may do: he may not impose on his fellows,—perhaps not on himself. Thus much *let* a man do: confidently and heartily live up to his thought. . . ."[33]

The self must be truly, confidently independent. Thoreau's self went a step further—away from civility, toward wildness. True, Hawthorne rather thought that "the high and classic cultivation in him" should be remarked in his talk of "all this wild freedom,"[34] but Thoreau himself took distinct pride in growing "savager and savager every day, as if fed on raw meat, and [as if] my tameness is only the repose of untamableness."[35]

There are, as Thoreau saw the state, two attractive features in wildness. The first is the source whence it comes, nature itself. As he put it:

It is in vain to dream of a wildness distant from ourselves. There is none such. It is the bog in our brain and bowels, the primitive vigor of Nature in us, that inspires that dream. I shall never find in the wilds of Labrador any greater wildness than in some recess in Concord, i.e., than I impart into it.[36]

[27]

Nature, then, is on the side of wildness; only sterile civilizations oppose it or seek to tame it. And where a choice has to be made, nature is to be trusted. The second attraction of wildness, on the other hand, more intimately connects with Thoreau's notion of the independent self. If society is tame, then the wild man is free. If the community is civilized, then the individualist alone appreciates the savage. If cultivated men walk one path and cut one kind of furrow, the primitive walks and cuts another. His differentness, the uniqueness of his self, indeed may be summed up as wildness:

> There is in my nature, methinks, a singular yearning toward all wildness. I know of no redeeming qualities in myself but a sincere love for some things, and when I am reproved, I fall back on to this ground. What have I to do with plots? I cut another furrow than you see.[37]

Here we have the secret of the free, wild self: "another furrow than you see." Thoreau not only seems different; he is different. Moreover, he suggests that, however you may act, however you may look, what really distinguishes your self from all other selves is something not visible, not measurable. Like other men, you will plow. Unlike other men, the field in which you work, the direction you take, and even the hand which guides the machine are not tangible. You grow up to selfhood, you become your own self, when you stop trying to measure your furrow by the dimensions of somebody else's customary cut.

Nevertheless, in the nature of things as they are, the instrumentation of cutting will have to be the same for one as for another. That is, the self one is, or would wish to be, has both bodily roots and spiritual aspirations; it will have one kind of relationship to the selves of others, another kind to the great self of nature; and in general it will trace its origins to and locate its destiny in the Universal One (under the name of God, Brahma, or

Over Soul). Therefore, the tool cannot be different, although its use may be.

Thoreau was insistent that his self was, initially if not primarily, a bodily self. Somewhat in the manner of Whitman, though less self-consciously, he asserted the claims of his body and its senses to a society either too prudish or too Platonic to acknowledge the propriety of either. "I stand in awe of my body," he said, "this matter to which I am bound has become so strange to me. . . . I fear bodies, I tremble to meet them. . . . Talk of mysteries! Think of our life in nature . . . the *solid* earth, the *actual* world, the *common* sense! Contact. Contact. *Who* are we? *Where* are we?"[38] We are, indeed, sentient selves. Our bodies are "all sentient. As I go here or there, I am tickled by this or that I come in contact with, as if touched by the wires of a battery."[39] We are animalistic in the sense that "a man can't ask properly for a piece of bread and butter without some animal spirits,"[40] no matter what the prudish and the timid may think. We are naturalistic in the sense that "as much depends on the state of the bowels as of the stars."[41]

Insofar as we are these things, our selves owe much to our bodies and senses—a debt that should be repaid, Thoreau believed, with common enthusiasm and uncommon conviction. What is our genius, he reminded us, but "the abundance of life or health, so that whatever addresses the senses . . . intoxicates with a healthy intoxication?"[42] And how can our selves be made whole and healthy unless we accord to body its rightful place in the hierarchy of our being? "I never feel that I am inspired unless my body is also. It too spurns a tame and commonplace life. . . . The body is the first proselyte the Soul makes."[43]

The body, then, together with a recognition of its claims, is important to the self—and to an understanding of the self. But so also is the soul, whether defined in a religious–philosophical sense or seen simply in terms of, let us say, the theory behind the facts of life, the essence beyond existence. "I find an instinct in me," Thoreau said, "conducting to a mystic spiritual life,"[44] an "instinct

toward a higher, or, as it is named, spiritual life."[45] This
instinct takes several forms: simple consciousness ("If
with closed ears and eyes I consult consciousness for a
moment, immediately are all walls and barriers dis-
sipated, earth rolls from under me, and I float"[46]); an
aspiration for that which lies beyond the senses ("I find
the actual to be far less real to me than the imagined. . . .
In proportion as to that which possesses my thoughts is
removed from the actual, it impresses me"[47]); and a preference for the ideal ("I am sane only when I have risen
above my common sense. . . . What is that other kind of
life to which I am thus continually allured? which alone
I love? Is it a life for this world?"[48]).

The giving in to this allurement not only expresses the
self and is an expression of the self but is yet another
way to "cut another furrow than you see." For it is not
common practice to give in; nor is it practical. But it does
individuate the self as perhaps few other activities may:

> My practicalness is not to be trusted to the last. To
> be sure, I go upon my legs for the most part, but,
> being hard-pushed and dogged by a superficial com-
> mon sense which is bound to near objects by beaten
> paths, I am off the handle, as the phrase is,—I
> begin to be transcendental and show where my
> heart is.[49]

Lest this expression of an advantage to the self in giving
in to the allurements of the spirit seem too vague, moreover, he cites certain other advantages of a more specific
sort: those of increasing "the susceptibleness of my nature
to noble impulses"[50]; of ministering to the possibility of
and capacity for wonder ("I am in rapture at my own
shadow. What if the substance were of as ethereal a nature?"[51]); and of enabling a mature man, as does a youthful one, to fulfill himself by climbing outside himself:

> Ah, those youthful days! Are they never to return?
> when the walker does not too curiously observe par-
> ticulars, but sees, hears, scents, tastes, and feels only

himself—the phenomena that show themselves in him—his expanding body, his intellect and heart. No worm or insect, quadruped or bird, confined his view, but the unbounded universe was his.[52]

Now although man's vision of the universe, that is, his youthful way of looking at the universe, should be unbounded. Thoreau of course recognized two boundaries to the self which existence in the universe imposed. These are the relationships which the self enjoys, or must suffer, to the natural world of living nature and to the artificial world of a less than vital human society. The one liberates and otherwise gives life to the self; the other confronts, constrains, and inhibits the self, if it does not actually kill it.

In filling out a questionnaire for the Association for the Advancement of Science dealing with his "philosophy," Thoreau said that to call himself a transcendentalist with respect to nature would be the simplest and yet (to a scientist) least understandable way of identifying his beliefs. "How absurd," he said, "that though I probably stand as near to nature as any of them, and am by constitution as good an observer as most, yet a true account of my relation to nature should excite their ridicule only."[53] This is because it was essentially a spiritual relation poetically expressed. There was some aestheticism to it: "Every landscape which is dreary enough has a certain beauty to my eyes."[54] Again, "There is nothing more affecting and beautiful to man, a child of earth, than the sight of the naked soil in the spring. I feel a kindredship with it."[55] There was even some fundamental, elemental Lucretianism to the relationship: "Shall I not have intelligence with the earth? Am I not partly leaves and vegetable mold myself?"[56] And certainly there was to be found in it the satisfying source of one of his most basic needs: "that sweet solitude my spirit seemed so early to require."[57] Primarily, however, the meaning and use of the self–nature relationship for Thoreau should be located in the imaginative and moral spheres. In nature his self broadened and deepened into selfhood. Everything in nature corresponded to and complemented the essence of this self. For example, the very patterns of nature helped to establish his own integrity:

> These regular phenomena of the seasons get at last to be . . . simply and plainly phenomena or phases of my life. The seasons and all their changes are in me. I see not a dead eel or floating snake or a gull but it rounds my life, like a line or accent in a poem.[58]

Moreover, to become acquainted with, to know well, to come to love nature's creatures would add dimension to his humanity, not merely depth to his science, because "I am the wiser in respect to all knowledges, and the better qualified for all fortunes, for knowing that there is a minnow in the brook. Methinks I have need even of his sympathy, and to be his fellow in a degree."[59] Finally, as Thoreau saw it anyway, to have this kind of relationship, which was surely a way of "cutting another furrow than you see," must mean not that the ideal self should become a "slave of matter" but that it alone would be capable of comprehending nature in the ideal way. For "this curious world which we inhabit is more wonderful than it is convenient, more beautiful than it is useful; it is more to be admired and enjoyed than used."[60]

On the other hand, Thoreau's self had far from an ideal relationship with human society. In fact, the trouble with society was that it was real, much too real. He claimed to have an "instinct for society" but noted with regret "an interval between my ideal and the actual," the trouble being that a real society could not "extend" him.[61] He was willing to admit that in part the fault was his, as when he said: "How poor and cold does Nature look, when, where we had expected to find a glassy lake, . . . we find only dull white ice. Such as I, no doubt, to my friends."[62] But the real difficulty lay with others, one might almost say with the nature of otherness. He complained that he could "treat his fellow as a god but receive less regard" from his fellow.[63] That is one thing.

A more important thing is that his fellow could do little for him:

> What is any man's discourse to me if I am not sensible of something in it as steady and cheery as the creak of crickets? In it the woods must be relieved against the sky. Men tire me when I am not constantly greeted and refreshed as by the flux of sparkling streams. Surely joy is the condition of life.[64]

Lastly, friends and neighbors are a temptation not only to neglect nature, the major source of this joy, but to forsake one's primary duty—of "cutting another furrow than you see"—and first purpose in life: to discover the self. Too often, he regretted, we are "apt to neglect the study of our own characters, thoughts, and feelings, and for the purpose of forming our own minds, look to others, who should merely be considered as different editions of the same great work."[65]

The self of Thoreau, then, is a self-conscious, self-assertive, and even self-contradictory entity. It loved and hated with equal intensity. It was attracted to and repelled by Concord and America. It was by turns stoic and epicurean, transcendental and naturalistic, scientific and poetic, public and private. It had its faults and confessed to them (in fact it put them forth as a kind of negative counsel). It had its virtues, but suggested ultimately that other selves discover their own graces. As it understood itself, it could be mean but at least it aspired to the heroic and the noble—by way of individualism, wildness, and an original relationship with nature. It knew the defeats of loneliness, sickness, death, and failure, but it was capable of strong psychological recoveries. It was a complete self, and it helped Thoreau to be his own man. That is also the lesson it holds forth to other men.

However, as he well knew, to be one's own man is or should be a means in life, not an end. "Cutting another furrow than you see," honest and admirable as it may be, is only the beginning of a man's destiny. Before the frontier of the soul closes, lest wildness become civility, independence turn into servility, and the summer of intuition become the winter of cold intellect, the self must have a precise and profound sense of purpose.

This Thoreau had. This he proposed to demonstrate to a dispirited, dispiriting public.

Chapter 3

PRIMACY OF PURPOSE:
"LET DEEP ANSWER TO DEEP"

A wise man will know what game to play today, and play it. Nothing must be postponed. Take time by the forelock. Now or never. You must live in the present, launch yourself on every wave, find your eternity in each moment.[1]

I go forth to make new demands on life. I wish to begin this summer well; to do something in it worthy of it and of me; to transcend my daily routine; to have my immortality now.[2]

The characteristic and often misunderstood perverseness of Thoreau is nowhere better illustrated than in his relaxed–profound, sweet–sour, rambling–taut dissertation on "Walking."[3] In it he gracefully, innocently converts an avocation, or mere pastime, into a vocation, or serious life's work. Taking the form of a familiar essay, which rarely in the history of the genre instructs more than it entertains, or has a purpose beyond that of giving aesthetic satisfaction, "Walking" easily invites the reader into a responsive, responsible discussion of that most important consideration: the need to discover and to develop a sense of purpose in life. The author seems to wander, aimlessly if pleasantly, but in his way he is driving toward a significant concept. Moreover, he seems to be meaning

nothing in particular, whereas he is actually positing the
sum of all his meanings.

Where should we walk? he opens. Why, naturally, in
"the fields and woods. What would become of us, if we
walked only in a garden or mall?" And what is a walk?
It is "a sort of crusade, preached by some Peter the
Hermit in us, to go forth and reconquer this Holy Land
from the hands of the infidels." How should we accou-
ter ourselves? In a "chivalric and heroic spirit which once
belonged to the rider" and is now to be found in "not the
knight, but walker, errant . . . a sort of fourth estate,
outside of Church and State and People." Above all, what
should be our gait? That of sauntering.

So far Thoreau has presented an interesting, imaginative metaphor. It is more than that. Not farfetched in the
least, it speaks directly to his point. The word "saunter" is
his point and purpose—not alone in this essay but in
his total philosophic program.

Walking, for Thoreau and for many in his Concord
audience, was a way of life. But there is an art to taking
walks, that being "the genius, so to speak, for sauntering."
Etymologically, he tells us, the word derived from the
beggars who, under the pretense of going to the Holy
Land, or *Sainte Terre,* wandered rather less nobly (or
so it would appear) about Europe, living from hand to
mouth, engaged in no purposeful activity, contributing
nothing to society, wasting time and their own individual
talents. He also suggests that the word might mean *"sans
terre,"* without land or home.

Thoreau finds two good senses in these etymologies.
One is that "they who never go to the Holy Land in their
walks, as they pretend, are indeed mere idlers and vaga-
bonds; but they who do go there are saunterers in the
good sense." The other is that it may not be a bad thing
at all "having no particular home"—provided this means
that saunterer-walkers are "equally at home everywhere."
Understanding these good senses, the reader no longer
deals with mere metaphor. He is, rather, getting on to
Thoreau's meaning, which is the idea of purpose.

To realize which land is holy is part of the meaning.

To appreciate, not paradoxically but precisely, that apparent purposelessness can be purpose-filled is another part. Such realizations lead to nothing less than the "secret of successful sauntering," whereas "he who sits still in a house all the time may be the greatest vagrant of all; but the saunterer . . . is no more vagrant than the meandering river . . . seeking the shortest source to the sea."

The good saunterer "walks like a camel," ruminating the while. He seeks nothing but finds much, for "an absolutely new prospect is a great happiness, and I can still get this any afternoon." He goes unencumbered, an interloper, because "the best part of the land is not private property. . . . The landscape is not owned." He is both generous in his poverty and casual in his dedication, because "to enjoy a thing exclusively is commonly to exclude yourself from the true enjoyment of it. Let us improve our opportunities, then, before the evil days come."

These opportunities lie about us. Therefore, "walk toward Oregon, and not toward Europe." Discover them in rural America, not in her great centers of civilization, and appreciate "that Adam in paradise was [not] more favorably situated on the whole than the backwoodsman in this country." Indeed, the more rural, the wilder the setting for your real (or symbolic) walk, the greater will be its opportunities:

> I wish to speak a word for Nature, for absolute freedom and wildness as contrasted with a freedom and culture merely civil—to regard man as an inhabitant, or a part and parcel of Nature, rather than as a member of society. I wish to make an extreme statement, if so I may make an emphatic one, for there are enough champions of civilization.[4]

The counsel of opportunity continues. Seek out and believe in "the forest and in the meadow, and in the night in which the corn grows," not in cities or the busy daylight activities of city-dwellers. Require an "infusion of hemlock spruce or arbor-vitae" in your tea, not a spot of brandy. Decide for the swamp. Elect a wildness "whose glance no civilization can endure." Become awake to all the sources of inspiration to which the sleep of duty-bound civilization has blinded us. Take a walk (his sense), forget about crusades (society's sense).

Clearly, Thoreau has stopped talking about walking, has "sauntered" into a discussion of intention, resolve, and resolution. More, he well understood that his private meanings had set him apart ("How vain, then, have been all your labors, citizens, for me!"), had made him into a holy outlaw not unlike the beggars of Europe, and had provided him with a gospel he would preach in the fashion of a new-style Peter the Hermit:

> If you are ready to leave mother and father and brother and sister and wife and child and friends, and never see them again,—and if you have paid your debts, and made your will, and settled all your affairs, and are a free man, then you are ready for a walk.[5]

Such a gospel contradicts the Protestant ethic and reverses the duty–pleasure principle. By it, the fool, the loafer, becomes a genius because he alone follows "the light which makes the darkness visible, like the lightning's flash, which perchance shatters the temple of knowledge itself." It calls a man away from evil routine and to holy leisure, enabling him thereby to find real purpose in his deliverance from false purposes. It is a sacred scripture pointing to "atmospheres unknown to my feet . . . to sympathy with Intelligence" itself.

Sturdy, steady citizens hear no such gospel, take no such walks. They "hug the earth." They "rarely mount." In their trips from business to bank they do not saunter. They know not the Holy Land. And, purposeful as they may seem, they really have no purpose. To these good citizens (but poor livers) Thoreau delivers this warning, this call to higher purposes than they have imagined:

We cannot afford not to live in the present. He is
blessed over all mortals who loses no moment of the
passing life in remembering the past. Unless our philosophy hears the cock crow in every barn-yard
within our horizon, it is belated.[6]

The *carpe diem* quality of such an admonition, one
which saunterers will heed more quickly than business-
men, is the first chartertistic of Thoreau's notion of
purpose. It is one which is deeply imbedded, not so much
in simple impatience, but in a personal sense of urgency.
Again and again he chides and goads himself: "I feel ripe
for something, yet do nothing, can't discover what that
thing is. I feel fertile merely. It is seedtime with me. I
have lain fallow long enough."[7] Or, "I don't want to feel
as if my life were a sojourn any longer. . . . It is time
now that I begin to live."[8] Or, "I will not let the years
roll over me like a Juggernaut car."[9] Or, "O make haste,
ye gods, with your winds and rains, and start the jam
before it rots."[10]

We should read these instigations as extending beyond
the limits of mere self-dissatisfaction. They reach to all
men who delay in time or who underestimate the possibilities inherent in their immediate situation. Purpose demands a response to the here and now. What is the use
of studying history, Thoreau wants to know, "if the ages
and generations are now?"[11] Why content ourselves
with the deceptively reassuring comforts of tradition
and routine when these are truly seen as inhibitions to
vital living? Instead, we should realize that "conscience,
if that be the name of it, was not given us for no purpose
or for a hindrance. However flattering order and ex-
pediency may look, it is but the repose of a lethargy,
and we will choose rather to be awake."[12]

But to awake to dreams—or chimeras—avails little.
To see purposeful action as spatially distant is as much
a mistake as to see it as temporally remote. Thoreau
points out that "it is good policy to be stirring about your
affairs, for the reward of activity and energy is that if
you do not accomplish the object you had proposed for

yourself, you do accomplish something else."[13] The great thing is to see either the object or the something else at the end of one's nose or the tips of one's fingers, wherever one happens to be, whatever one happens to be doing. Forget about "the momentous topics of human life," he advises; these "are always of secondary importance to the business at hand."[14] Attempt "to harvest the crop which [your] life yields," whatever it may be. Don't strain to reach apples or oranges if that crop "yields only ground nuts." In such an instance the best advice about purpose is—dig, don't soar.[15] The reason is that one should "dwell as near as possible to the channel in which your life flows," it being essential, therefore, "that a man confine himself to pursuits . . . which lie next to and conduce to his life, which do not go against the grain, either of his will or his imagination."[16] In short, "Go not so far out of your way for a truer life. . . . Do the things which lie nearest you."[17] For the beginning of a sense of purpose is the realization that a "more substantial life" or "glorious experience" is not over there—but here.

There was, however, a certain prudence tempering the urgency which we find in Thoreau's cry for action in the here and now. Indeed, the second characteristic of a sense of purpose may be described as deliberateness. This is not as contradictory as it may sound. In fact, the explanation may be as simple and reasonable as an awareness of making haste slowly. Having a proper reverence for life and convinced that "one moment of life costs many hours," Thoreau was willing to take time away from business or social activity in order to give that one moment hours of "preparation and invitation."[18] This is to say that leisure is one's business. Moreover, deliberateness of action is a way of preparing oneself for the essentials of leisure. For this reason, "nothing can be more useful to a man than a determination not to be hurried. . . . I cannot think nor utter my thoughts unless I have infinite room."[19] In this regard, as in several others, Thoreau definitely aligns himself with the Oriental "who has nothing to do in this world" rather than with the Oc-

cidental who "is full of activity." For deliberately, pur-
posely, to contemplate the sun makes more sense than
"to hasten toward the sunset."[20] It is to "take a position outside the street and daily life of men." It is to plan
your own course, not to do your neighbor's business. It
is to engage in "only absorbing employment," calmly,
independently, with an unhurried sense that you find
both meaning and pleasure in what you do—and wish to
have the time in which to savor both. Thus is purpose
deliberate: slow only in that society finds you "not doing
anything," rapid enough for you to pluck your own flower of the day.[21]

Purpose, then, begins in immediacy but is maintained
deliberately. To bring it to ripeness the man of purpose
must present three attributes: seriousness, spiritual youthfulness, and practicality.

Seriousness is not the same thing as morbidity but it is
related to an appreciation of life's somber side. Without
it, one tends to be frivolous—and so to miss life's opportunities by underestimating their potency. With it, one
puts a just estimate on whatever comes up. As Thoreau
remarked, "There is a certain fertile sadness which I
would not avoid, but rather earnestly seek. It is positively joyful to me. It saves my life from being trivial."[22]
The serious man, like the saint, must learn to die, to fall,
to fail, and especially to lose—because in defeat and loss
there is gain: "Not till we are lost, in other words, not
till we have lost the world, do we begin to find ourselves,
and realize where we are and the infinite extent of our
relations."[23] Maintaining himself "in whatever attitude he
finds himself through obedience to the laws of his being,"[24] dead to the world and yet painfully aware of its
tragedy, the serious man does not regard "the human
journey" as the dilettante regards traveling—as a pastime.
"It is as serious as the grave," rather, "and it requires a
long probation to be broken into it."[25]

This sounds like the talk of an old, or at least a mature, man. But Thoreau also stood up for the sentiments and attitudes of youth, especially when he was discussing the necessity of having purpose in life. It is the

old who are tired, dispirited, apathetic. It is the young whose energy derives as much from conviction as from health and hope. "The young man," he said, "is a demigod; the grown man, alas, is commonly a mere mortal. He is but half here. . . ."[26] The young man has the kind of animal drive that purpose requires of all men. He is "athletic, active, beautiful. Then, too, his thoughts will be like his person. . . . If you are well, then how brave you are. . . . You are conversant with joy. A man thinks as well through his legs and arms as his brain."[27] Moreover, it is the young, the very young alone, who know how to get the most out of life because they bring the best possible motives to it. That is, their purpose is to enjoy it. Thoreau expressed the notion quite incisively in contrasting the motives of professional (commercial) and amateur (the root meaning of the word is "love") berrypickers:

If it were left to the berries to say who should have them, is it not likely that they would prefer to be gathered by the party of children in the hayrigging, who have come to have a good time merely?[28]

With the young, then, Thoreau associated two qualities which he felt could not be divorced from a proper sense of purpose: bodily vigor and a capacity for enjoyment. He knew or cared not what others might think but he knew that his dark days came when he lacked either quality and therefore lacked purpose. When he did something about the lack, he could—purposefully—save himself: "I was going to sit and write or mope all day in the house, but it seems wise to cultivate animal spirits, to embark in enterprises which employ and recreate the whole body."[29] When he could not do anything about the lack, his regret was as strong as his aimlessness: "There was a time when the beauty and the music were all within, and I sat and listened to my thoughts, and there was a song in them."[30] For to be young is to run for nothing, to sing for fun, and to pick berries for their own sake. Such as do these things have discovered a pur-

pose in life. More to the point at issue, their youthfulness
has brought purpose to life.

As for the connection of practicality with purpose in
Thoreau's scheme, suffice it to say that his view of the
matter was impishly typical. Others might think of purpose in abstract, high-sounding, essentially moral terms,
but he tended to reduce its stature without at the same
time restricting its dimension. He was perpetually interested in the small and insignificant. Persons like farmers
Minotte and Rice and Melvin and Goodwin were as important to him as Socrates, Christ, or Shakespeare, and
infinitely more important than politicians or tradesmen—
because in their own way they did what they had to do,
however mean the "what" seemed. As he put it, "I
see Melvin all alone filling his sphere . . . which no other
could fill or suggest. He takes up as much room in nature
as the most famous."[31] Obviously, Melvin filled his sphere
in a very practical way: hoeing, milking, mending fences.
He didn't make the newspapers and he won't make the
history books, but he had a business and he did it, his
own business, and "in spite of Malthus and the rest,
there will be plenty of room in this world, if every man
will mind his own business."[32] But, as with persons, so
also with business. Thoreau will ground it. "You must be
able to extract nutriment out of a sand heap,"[33] he
said. There is as much purpose in that business as in proposing philosophies or building empires. Moreover, in answer to a question about useful philosophies and schemes
which might become a man's purpose (and be becoming
to it), he answered most emphatically:

> Why not make a very large mud-pie and bake it in
> the sun! Only put no Church nor State into it, nor
> upset any other pepper-box that way. Dig out a wood-
> chuck,—for that has nothing to do with rotting insti-
> tutions. Go ahead.[34]

Go ahead—in the direction of nature. That is the
point of the command. Thoreau's idea of purpose has to
mean that. Nature, after all, was the place in which he

had discovered his own purpose as well as, or so he
thought, the source of purpose itself. It was here that he
conducted his serious, youthful, practical business: to
analyze a bird's nest, to chart a lake, to examine animal
excrement, to watch a hawk, to measure a snowfall. Here
he composed odes to spring, arrowheads, and berrying;
elegies on fallen trees, the sociology of chipmunks, the
philosophy of trout. Nature was his background, and "all
our lives want a suitable background. They should at
least, like the life of the anchorite, be as impressive to
behold as objects in the desert, a broken shaft or crum-
bling mound against a limitless horizon."[35] Against such
a setting a man could find out who he was and what he
was for—by measuring himself against the fundamental
and the monumental. Amid the art and artifacts of civilization, man loses his sense of proportion. For this reason
"our village life would stagnate if it were not for the un-
explored forests and meadows which surround it."[36] Stag-
nating, we need to be stirred up, refreshed, recreated—
to be given anew a sense of purpose: "It is important,
then, that we should air our lives from time to time by
removals, and excursions into the fields and woods—starve
our vices. So do not sit so long over any cellar-hole as to
tempt your neighbor to bid for the privilege of digging
saltpeter there."[37] Society is a privy, a cistern of body-
waste. Nature is an invitation to renewal. When renewed,
then and only then can man be receptive to those principles which Thoreau thought basic to a maintaining as
well as an initial discovery of purpose: serenity and acceptance. An example of what he meant by the former,
which he termed "biblical and no man's invention" and
which he interpreted as a natural man's social reaction
to the circumstances of his life, would be in the question
and answer that, he says, Tartars exchange in greeting:

Q. Have your mares been fruitful?
A. All is at peace in our pasture.[38]

In Thoreau's view, men talk that way because they live
that way. "How are you?—I'm fine," on the other hand,

is unrevealing talk reflecting purposeless lives, the lives of the dull, not the serene. As for acceptance, the object lesson is to be taken from the manner in which nature encompasses her brute creatures, and how these in turn, unthinking, unstriving, find their meaning by yielding to the perfect whole of nature. One example out of many possible would be his expressed admiration for the way in which a stray dog, as against busy townspeople, reacted to fall foliage: "He trotted down the yard as if it were a matter of course after all, or else as if he deserved it all."[39]

Concordians and Americans may learn from Tartars and stray dogs to be natural. But they "must be something more than natural,—even supernatural. Nature will not speak through but along with them."[40] They must be as serene as life on the plains, as passive as the falling of leaves. This is a portion of purpose. Another portion, however, demands that they probe: "We are surrounded by a rich and fertile mystery. May we not probe it, pry into it, employ ourselves about it, a little?"[41] This life is "our portion of the infinite," and it is our task, using nature as a vantage point, to look up after we have looked around. Commenting on animal tracks in the snow, Thoreau gives us the direction: "Are we not cheered by the sight? And does not all this amount to the track of a higher life . . . ?" Have mortals lost the scent, failing to detect "a trace of intelligence" in the elemental? The suggested corrective, itself a masterly lesson in purpose, is to live a life which "pursued, does not earth itself, does not burrow downward—but upward."[42]

Indeed, there is purpose in the particular and the practical—but only if one is able to see the general in the particular, the universal theory (higher laws? superior intelligence? Supreme Being? Pure Thought? The Idea and The Ideal?) beyond the practical fact. Thoreau's mentor, Ellery Channing, once observed: "I am universal. I have nothing to do with the particular and the definite." Thoreau agreed: "I, too, would set down something besides facts. Facts should be only as the frame to my pictures. . . . My facts shall be falsehoods to the common sense. I would so state facts that they shall be significant, shall be myths or mythologies."[43] Facts, even natural facts, may help a man to purpose; kept on a low level, however, they may interfere with that purpose. As Thoreau complained: "Latterly, I have heard the very flies buzz too distinctly, and have accused myself because I did not still the superficial din. We must not be too easily distracted by the crying of children or of dynasties."[44] The man of purpose, then, will hold himself aloof, keep himself pure, strive for the infinite arising out of the finite, seek to discover the ideal beyond the real:

> We seek too soon to ally the perceptions of the mind to the experience of the hand, to prove our gossamer truths practical, to show their connection with everyday life (better show their distance from our everyday life), to relate them to the cider mill and the banking institution. Ah, give me pure mind, pure thought.[45]

However much Thoreau believed in or aspired to this "pure thought," the fact is that he positively put forth a more efficacious, more realizable thought, one which was not systematic but which nevertheless had some system to it, one which was more of a moral theology than an intellectual philosophy, and one which may be regarded as his credo—that is, not a profession of faith, but a full, final statement of purpose.

This statement represents his "wisdom," and "wisdom does not inspect but behold. We must look a long time before we can see."[46] He saw. What he saw he set forth for our beholding. Modestly but truthfully, he would have us behold a philosopher, with the understanding that we read the term in this way: "To be a philosopher is not merely to have subtle thoughts, nor even to found a school, but so to love wisdom as to live according to its dictates, a life of simplicity, independence, magnanimity, and trust."[47] Further, he would have us understand that the message of this philosopher is not complete, cannot be made whole, and yet is offered as a guide to life. What he said of and for himself as well holds true for his readers across the years:

> I yet lack discernment to distinguish the whole lesson of today; but it is not lost,—it will come to me at last. My desire is to know *what* I have lived, that I may know *how* to live henceforth.[48]

To put this another way, just as he set down facts in his journal, not to find out what he had done, but to learn "what I am and aspire to become," so also does he recommend to the student of his philosophy the discovery of purpose in "a record of experiences and growth, not a preserve." These should bespeak and betoken "not a maturity" but "a certain greenness, though freshness."[49]

Being is a becoming. Purpose is a developing. Fair enough. But what were his counsels, one might say commandments, by which these ongoing processes could be directed? They were eight: proportion, economy, vitality, vigor, hope, resolve, love, and conviction. Each is an aspect of his philosophy; all add up to the primacy of purpose in his view of life.

1. *Proportion.* As early as his part in the Commencement proceedings at Harvard College, Thoreau had argued against "the commercial spirit," the origins of which he located "in a blind and unmanly love of wealth," because as a "ruling spirit" it tended to dominate life, thus to throw it out of balance. The philosophic man of purpose, however, possessed of a sense of proportion, could restore the balance by a simple, dramatic act (one which in effect Thoreau performed many times), which would signify the true value of things. Such an act could be, he suggested, to work but one day a week and to enjoy the leisure of "six sabbaths."[50] Thus would sauntering through life become a holy crusade. Thus, too, would the ruling spirit, or at least the code by which one lived, be brought into line with the essential values of life. Quite simply, proportion reduces itself to this: work to live, don't live to work.

2. *Economy.* There is so much waste in and of human life that mankind would be well advised to follow the model of natural objects, such as a willow tree, to conserve one's resources. As Thoreau hoped, "May I ever be in as good spirits as a willow! How tenacious of life! How withy! How soon it gets over its hurts! It never despairs." What is its secret? Why, it is to transmit all of its wounds into sap, which then becomes the source of its renewal.[51] Men expend themselves, wasting their strength beyond the point of recovery, losing the value of their defects and defections. Thoreau's message to them is not the sentimental, grandiose "to strive, to seek, to find, but not to yield." Rather it is a counsel of earthy, earthly tenacity, of survival by roots, and of economical use and re-use of one's own natural resources.

3. *Vitality.* We get bogged down, Thoreau thought. Things which don't matter occupy us. Worse, they destroy us. Important things we put off. The contest is thus between living and dying, between the gain of vitality and the loss of apathy. Therefore, choose life. "Are we more than crepuscular in our intellectual and spiritual life? Have we awakened to broad noon? The morning hope is soon lost in what becomes the routine of the day. . . ."[52] The letter (of the law, of custom, of regulations, of codes, of routine) kills, but the spirit (of imagination, of adventure, of experimentation, of doing what one wills) gives life.

4. *Vigor.* Let us not think too much, or think "too precisely on't." There is a strength in us we have not dreamed of. It is in our bodies. Recognizing this, "we need pray for no higher heaven than the pure senses can furnish, a purely sensuous life."[53] Thoreau does not deny the existence of pure thought, of an ideal beyond the senses. He does feel that too often the striving for pure thought is done at the expense of life, this life. Moreover, he believes that the way to the suprasensuous is the way of the senses.

5. *Hope.* Each man, however poorly situated, has much to live for. He encourages himself—and his neighbors—if he puts forth and emphasizes his strength rath-

er than his weaknesses: "We should impart our courage, and not our despair, our health and ease, and not our disease."[54] Joy is the condition of life. Hope is as hope does.

6. *Resolve.* As time must be "taken by the forelock," so must purpose. Irresolution is as much a natural sin as delay. The time is now. The call is for decision: "Will you live? Or will you be embalmed? Will you break your heart, your soul, to save your neck? Necks and pipestems are fated to be broken."[55]

7. *Love.* If it is your purpose to enjoy, then it is your duty to give joy. "Cold resolve begets nothing." But "to yield to love"[56] is to fulfill one's own nature—by enhancing the natures of one's fellows.

8. *Conviction.* The perfection of purpose, like the crown of life, will be found within, not without. One's goal should be, out of a supremely confident attitude and sense of one's own rightness and righteousness, to get life to conform to the interior, intuited ideal, not to shape one's ideals by externals. Therefore, "Obey the law which reveals, and not the law revealed."[57]

These were his counsels. Without them, he felt, men would seek purpose without purpose. With them, nothing less than meaning in life was possible. He knew that the world (life, if you will) "is a cow that is hard to milk,—life does not come so easy,—and oh, how thinly it is watered ere we get it!"[58] He knew that, like horses on a treadmill, the purposeless man, "symbolical of the moral condition" of most of humanity, lived as a brute beast, as artisan only, "in contradistinction from artists."[59] And he knew that most people, even his dearest friends and closest neighbors, would completely misunderstand his idea of purpose, mistaking it for indolence or indecision ("And there that darned fool had been standin'— the livelong day—a-studyin'—the habits of the bullfrog."[60]

He knew. He didn't care. For when systems failed and friends proved false, he could turn to nature and there find confirmation of his conviction, the very purpose of purpose. As he put it: "I have come to this hill to see the sun go down, to recover sanity and put myself again in relation with Nature. I would fain drink a draft of Nature's serenity. Let deep answer to deep."[61]

What he meant was that the "deep" in himself would correspond to and be complemented by the depth of nature. There he could justify an heroic Raleigh and a simple self. There he might learn to balance the need for immediacy with the caution of deliberateness. There he could be serious, and young, and practical out of his own deep—and expect another deep to ratify his foolish sauntering. There he could fashion a philosophy out of equal parts of matter and spirit—and be assured that the depths of ontology would bless him, even if a superficial logic would not. There, deep unto deep, he could both answer and sustain these essential questions, the very same ones that men of no purpose fail to answer—or fail to ask: Cannot society return to natural simplicity? Must mind and instinct be opposed? Should not civilization have something to gain from primitive sensuality? Is it not possible for a man to hold "perfect communion with Nature"?

Men of little or no purpose are ultimately identified as those who live on the surface of their own natures and on the surface of nature itself. It is their shallowness which renders them vagrant, impotent, erratic. But when "deep answers to deep," purpose is not only disclosed but proclaimed.

Those who do not or will not grasp this meaning, however, are doomed to defile life. It shall be the final purpose of a man of purpose to be able to identify and condemn the defilement.

PART II:

DEFLECTION

Chapter 4

DEFILEMENT OF LIFE:
"THE DEAD UNKIND"

All men are partially buried in the grave of custom, and of some we see only the crown of the head above ground. Better are they physically dead, for they more lively rot.[1]

How much of the world is widow's thirds, with a hired man to take negligent care of it.[2]

Prophets and poets are rarely satisfied, because, having had visions of the good life, they are particularly and peculiarly sensitive to that which is less than perfect, that which tends to defile whatever small good there may be. Both are as earnest in their endeavors to proclaim the best as they are to discern the merely meretricious. In fact, the positive in their message does not so much depend on as arise from the negative. Their common difficulty has always been a rhetorical one: how to persuade their generally insensible audiences that their plaints and complaints proceed from a belief in improvement, not from a conviction of despair; that they preach the possibility of reform, not an inexorable defection; and that they themselves are, as it were, happy opportunists, not wretched cranks.

Thoreau, mythologist of the good life and counselor to the dejected or simply confused, can be considered as prophet and poet facing the same rhetorical difficulties. He had a gospel to preach to unbelievers. Its thrust, taking off firmly from a sense of the self and the primacy of purpose, was sure and satisfactory as far as he was concerned. Would others find it so? If they could not, they must be told why not. If they could, they still must be

[53]

convinced of very real threats to their faith—especially
when they did not recognize them as threats. And if they
did not know what to believe or whom to disbelieve, perhaps they might be prodded awake by an exaggerated
jeremiad. Whoever they were, in whatever disposition,
they presented this problem for the rhetorician: How
could they be reached?

The solution to the problem, first effected by the Hebrew
prophets and later perfected by the English poets, was
to talk to men simply, in familiar terms, about concrete
objects, the existence of which they had taken for granted,
the moral implications of which, with the help of a warning, they could infer. Call it the methodology of insinua-
tion.

Thoreau had mastered this method, a striking example
of which may be read in his apparently innocuous, actually provocative meditation on "Wild Apples."[3] There is
a sting to his sweet words, and the defilers of life are
meant to suffer its pain.

How gently and plainly he opens his discourse, however, with a completely disarming account of the history
of the apple tree, its importance as a basic food, and its
singular recognition by the mythologists, the biblicists,
the classicists, and the poets—as well as by the botanists.
Theophrastus, Thoreau tells us, regarded it as "the most
civilized of all trees . . . harmless as a dove, as beautiful
as a rose, and as valuable as flocks and herds." Fortunately,
ancient man recognized its value, carrying it with him in
his wanderings from place to place and thus indirectly
providing a source of life not only to all the world's primitive and civilized peoples but also to "birds, quadrupeds,
and insects."

A basic food resource, the apple tree (Thoreau continues) is a source of beauty as well. The sight and smell
of it can be "enjoyed without robbing anybody." More
wonderfully, it has a "certain volatile and ethereal quality which represents [its] highest value, and which cannot
be vulgarized, or bought and sold." Mean men may pick
it and market it. Only "the godlike among men begin to
taste its ambrosial qualities."

It would appear that lesser mortals have always been antagonistic to "the fair and fragrant apples." But since it is "the noblest of fruit," only the "most beautiful or the swiftest, those who are able to accept this gift with more joy and gratitude," are really entitled to the harvest. True, the crass and sordid think that the harvest is theirs, seeking to despoil the apples by trading in them. Nor do they seem to realize that they cannot win the contest. A cart-man, for example,

> begins to lose his load the moment he tries to transport them to where they do not belong, that is, to any but the most beautiful. Though he gets out from time to time, and feels of them, and thinks they are all there, I see the stream of their evanescent and celestial qualities going to heaven from his cart, while the pulp and skin and core only are going to market.[4]

The benighted cart-man, like all mean men, sees the product in terms of produce. He would not be "grateful for Nature's bounty" unless he could traffic in it. Thus he seeks to visit his own debasement on the good of this world. But there are some innocently knowing souls who can appreciate it for what it is. These are "the wild only like myself, perchance, who belong not to the aboriginal race here, but have strayed into the woods from the cultivated stock." Such as these, the gentle savages, properly value the gift before them:

> Every wild apple shrub excites our expectation thus, somewhat as every wild child. It is, perhaps, a prince in disguise. What a lesson to man! So are human beings, referred to the highest standard, the celestial fruit which they suggest and aspire to bear, browsed on by fate; and only the strongest and most persistent genius defends itself and prevails, sends a tender scion upward at last, and drops its fruit on the ungrateful earth.[5]

As with the fruit, so with the fancier. It grows—against odds and with thorns ("to defend itself against foes").

In its thorniness, however, "there is no malice, only some malic acid." Its direction is confidently upward, darting there with joy, to defeat the depredations of cows—and meaner animals such as men. Suffering great hardships "to bear a sweet fruit," the apple tree is sustained largely by its mission. It survives because "it has not forgotten its high calling." Similarly, the man of "taste," he for whom the fact of a wild apple becomes a symbol, is and should be "hard to get at"; his virtues are protected by the thorniness of his nature, his joy transcends the sharpness of his rebukes (those he gives and those he suffers), his aspiration is ethereal, and his calling is above that of men—and cows.

These apples of Concord (not of Discord, Thoreau reminds us) are meant for the out-of-doors. Eaten there, they are "spirited and racy." Brought into the house, "they have a harsh and crabbed taste." Again, so it is with men. They were intended for a certain kind of life. When they live it, they are sweetly fulfilled. When it is denied them, or they deny it to themselves, they turn sour—and, souring, they poison the atmosphere. If it is true that the "era of the wild apple will soon be past," that "a century hence" he who walks over the fields will have to forgo elemental pleasures, that scientifically grafted trees and unsocially fenced orchards will one day mean that "we shall be compelled to look for our apples in a barrel . . . fit for diseased palates only," then it will also be true that, in the name of civilization, mankind will have suffered a tremendous loss: not of the fruit of the wild tree but of the fruit of the free spirit. Should this happen, men will wither and die—or else be good for barrels only. For what they have done to their apples they are inclined to do to themselves. Worse, in ruining themselves they would despoil life itself.

Thoreau closes his analogy with a powerfully apposite quotation from the opening verse of the *Book of Joel,* which was a lamentation, a call to reformation and repentance, a vision of what might have been and could still be, and a precise statement, although metaphorically phrased, of defilement:

This is the word of the Lord that came to Joel the son of Pethuel. Hear this, ye old men, and give ear. . . . That which the palmer worm hath left hath the locust eaten. . . . Awake, ye drunkards, and weep. . . . Be ye ashamed, O ye vinedressers. The vine is dried up, and the fig tree languisheth; the pomegranate tree, the palm tree also, and the apple tree, even all the trees of the field are withered: because joy is withered away from the sons of men.[6]

To Thoreau as to Joel, the terrible trouble is with man, not the fruits of earth. That is, it is not that man sorrows because the trees are blighted; it is, rather, that they are withered because man is withered. Who is man? What ails him? He is "a surly porter, or a vain and hectoring bully / Who can claim no nearer kindredship with me / Than brotherhood by law."[7] So offensive is he that Thoreau "almost shrinks from the arduousness of meeting [him] erectly by day."[8] Hearing no celestial music, he perforce grovels in "the dust and mire of the universe," and is best described therefore as "infidel," as "poor, timid, unenlightened, and thick-skinned," and as "hopelessly ignorant and unbelieving." It is no wonder, then, that given a world largely populated by creatures of this character, sensitive persons (Thoreau perhaps) are "ordinarily in a state of desperation; such is our life; oftentimes it drives us to suicide."[9] It is not that Thoreau, or so he says at any rate, has not tried to understand and hence to love his fellows. He has—only to discover that "of all phenomena, my own race are the most mysterious and undiscoverable. For how many years have I striven to meet one, even on common manly ground, and have not succeeded."[10] Indeed, his intellectual analysis of mankind keeps depressing him, keeps reminding him of "remissness": for "duties neglected, unfaithfulness, shamming, impurity, falsehood, inhumanity." If he could simply love without question or analysis, perhaps man would be more attractive to him. This he cannot do, however. One man suffers from as well as for the faults of all men. Moreover, "when the brain chiefly is nourished, and not the affections, seeds become merely excremental."[11]

Misanthropy? No more with Thoreau than with Joel or Jeremias. It would be easier and more pleasant merely to love. But there is a sickness in this fair world, the once and future paradise, and the sickness is man. Therefore, to probe painfully, precisely, and systematically to the root of the ailment is to be both just and kind—wise, too, if paradise is ever to be reclaimed.

Mankind, as Thoreau early determined, suffers from certain general, possibly even innate, flaws. He fails to appreciate the happy opportunities which lie about him: "That man who does not believe that each day contains an earlier, more sacred, and auroral hour than he has yet profaned, has despaired of life."[12] Losing the invigorating sense of daily challenge, he reduces living to the level of a forced labor camp: "It is hard to have a Southern overseer; it is worse to have a Northern one; but worst of all when you are the slave-driver of yourself."[13] Thus "a man may spend the whole of his life . . . accomplishing a particular design" but never "taking time to look around him and appreciate the phenomenon of his existence."[14] It is no wonder, then, that he lives "meanly and miserably":

> We escape fate continually by the skin of our teeth. . . . What kind of gift is life unless we have spirits to enjoy it? We should first of all be full of vigor like a strong horse. . . . Have the gods sent us into this world . . . to do chores . . . and not given us any spending money?[15]

No wonder—and also a tragedy, this "doing outrage" to one's proper nature, this performing "the office of inferior and brutal creatures. Hence come war and slavery in; and what else may not come in by this opening."[16]

Man is sick. But he also transmits his disease to the universe, infecting its atmosphere, impairing its natural course, defiling its presence and its promise. This is his general condition, the burden of his humanity. There are, however, more specific grievances against him, ones for which he is more personally responsible but with which he defiles his world just as surely. Thoreau identifies these as giving in to his herd instinct; living by custom and convention; erecting institutions; and overvaluing work. Man alone is bad enough. When he congregates, single troubles multiply. Thoreau, of course, had no love for crowds, especially the crowds in cities. In them men "assemble," not "associate."[17] In fact, as he saw it, the social virtue of "good fellowship" commonly practiced in the city was really only "the virtue of pigs in a litter, which lie close together to help each other keep warm."[18] He could see no advantage (moral, social, cultural) in urban life, claiming that "the only room in Boston which I visit with alacrity is the Gentlemen's Room at the Fitchburg Depot,"[19] and maintaining that its only use was a negative one:

I don't like the city better, the more I see it, but worse. I am ashamed of my eyes that behold it. . . . It will be something to hate—that's the advantage it will be to me. . . . The pigs in the street are the most respectable part of the population.[20]

Moreover, unlike simple rural settlements which are forever close to the lively, recreative sources of nature, cities have a way of being built atop the ruins of more ancient ones, "where the dwellings of the living are in the cemeteries of the dead, and the soil is blanched and accursed."[21] In such places there is no life, least of all for human beings who must inevitably become "natural mummies":

The life having departed out of them, decay and putrefaction, disorganization, has not taken place but they still keep up a dry and withered semblance of life.[22]

This death-in-life mode, which Thoreau felt was built into city life, was reason enough for him to shun it and to curse it. But there was another reason of which he would be peculiarly aware. It was that a city by definition and practice is an assemblage of people in crowds, not the home of individuals. Crowds repelled on several counts. One, "A crowd of men seems to generate vermin. . . . In great towns there is degradation undreamed of elsewhere,—gamblers, dog-killers, rag-pickers."[23] In other words, the morality of individuals becomes the immorality of masses. Two, given the nature of mankind, the best never improves the worst, with the result that the moral reform of crowds is virtually impossible: "The mass never comes up to the standard of its best member, but on the contrary degrades itself to a level with the lowest."[24] Three, whatever may be the talk of high civilization in the gathering of crowds in urban centers, it was Thoreau's belief that mass living meant, had to mean, enforced, anti-personal patterns of conduct and impositions of false standards: "It is unsafe to defer so much to mankind and the opinions of society, for these are always and without exception heathenish and barbarous."[25]

Sometimes these "opinions" are simply *ad hoc* oppositions to an individual's natively free and spontaneous instinct, the instinct for the good and abundant life itself. More often than not, however, these opinions crystallize, harden, even fossilize into the deadweight of custom and convention. When this happens, there is no instinct, for it must yield to the utterly stale routine of procedural living. This no free man can possibly accept:

> The life which society proposes to me to live is so artificial and complex—bolstered up on so many weak supports, and sure to topple down at last—that no man can ever be inspired to live it, and only "old fogies" praise it.[26]

Such a mechanized life kills the possibility of "infinite joy" and certainly impedes "the satisfaction of helping myself." It, too, results in a death-in-life, a living death from which even the freest, most lively spirits are not entirely spared. For "all men are partially buried in the grave of custom, and of some we see only the crown of the head above ground. Better are they physically dead, for they more lively rot."[27] Custom saps the vital spirit, then, quite frequently for no reason at all, or for no good reason. This is its foolishness, its insanity. Thoreau was apt to remark bitterly on this feature but he could make his point as well by gentle mockery. For example, he took the occasion of a visit to Quebec City, "protected" as it is by the Heights of Abraham, to comment on the common practice, set by convention, hallowed by custom, of building a wall about a settlement, then of having the guarding wall guarded by soldiers. As he put the matter, "What a troublesome thing a wall is! I thought it was to defend me, and not I it! Of course, if they had no wall, they would not have need to have any sentinels."[28] Just so, he thought. Man is not made for conventions; conventions are supposed to be made for him. But once he establishes one, he becomes trapped by his own folly —and perpetuates it.

Not satisfied with "hoisting himself up by his own petard" through the foolishness of habituated, habituating patterns of life, man goes one step further along the road to self-debasement and world defilement. He institutionalizes his life. He could worship as he pleases but he elects to establish formal religions. Why? Thoreau wishes to know. "Preaching? . . . Who are ye that ask for these things? What do ye want to hear, ye puling infants?" With his "thoughts in petticoats" and having "covenanted with a timid devil," he neither truly worships nor gets real value from his church: "It is Christianity bunged up."[29] He is free and able to govern himself but he elects to establish governments which rule him but do not reward him for his pains: "If you aspire to anything better than politics, expect no cooperation from men. They will not further anything good. You must prevail of your own force, as a plant springs and grows by its own vitality."[30] He is quite capable of thinking for himself but he elects to found or subscribe to schools of. thought which, the better organized and institutionalized they are, the more they restrain the freedom of his thought. Thus the school philosopher "girds himself for his enterprises with fastings and prayers, and then, instead of pressing forward like a light-armed soldier, with the fewest possible hindrances, he at once hooks himself on to some immovable institution. . . ."[31] He was destined by nature to live and to let live but he elects to clutter up and clot his life with useless absurdities, such as a leisure class, a philanthropic class, a dilettantish class, none of which could possibly do him any good, all of which he would have to support. Thoreau called such people "creatures covered with slime. The non-producers. How many of these bloodsuckers there are fastened to every helpful man? It is a world full of snivelling prayers, whose very religion is a prayer. As if beggars were admirable. . . . They cling like the glutton to a living man and suck his vitals up."[32]

All these institutions man elects—at his own expense, at the cost of his life. Some of them, Thoreau admitted, may have had "a divine origin. But of most that we see prevailing in society nothing but the form, the shell is left; the life is extinct, and there is nothing divine in them."[33] With life open to him, he closes himself off. With the possibility of life and yet more abundant life before him always, he opts for death. It is, then, with scorn and with sadness that Thoreau concludes: "I love mankind, but I hate the institutions of the dead unkind."[34]

Now what he hated chiefly about the "dead unkind" was their herdish, conventional institution of work, perhaps the deadliest and deadest of all man's odd inventions, surely the one which was most unkind to Thoreau's way of life. For work, as mankind elevated it and Thoreau rejected it, was a substitute for life.

He knew what it was to work, had (minimally) supported himself by work, and had even upon occasion worked for others. So he spoke out of conviction, not out of indolence. But modern society's idea of work, not to speak of its practices, went against his grain. Work did not, as many thought, rank with cleanliness next to godliness. Rather, "with most men life is postponed to some trivial business and so therefore is heaven." Indeed, it stands between man and his right to paradise, earthly or heavenly, in that "there is no glory so bright but the veil of business can hide it effectively."[35] Work has been made into a necessity of life, whereas Thoreau regarded it as trivial at the most. "What are the men of New England about?" he asked; "I have traveled some in New England, especially in Concord, and I have found that no enterprise was on foot which it would not disgrace a man to take part in."[36] Work does not add stature to a man, cannot mature him or make him noble. Instead it demeans him: "How trivial and uninteresting and wearisome and unsatisfactory are all employments for which men will pay you money. . . . You are paid for being something less than a man."[37] According to society, work is a portion of life, man's portion in life. According to Thoreau, work stands between man and his life, but "my life will wait for nobody . . . is being matured still without delay, while I go about the streets and chaffer with this man and that to secure it a living."[38] When all other arguments fail, then society proposes work, a doing of something, a doing of anything, as a way of morally disciplining a man, of keeping him in line. To this argument Thoreau responded plainly and severely: "If labor mainly . . . serves the purpose of a police, to help men out of mischief, it indicates a rottenness at the foundation of our community."[39]

Thoreau indicted all kinds of work (or at least the wrong attitude toward work itself) but reserved his most caustic comments for Concord's major work at the time, farming. Had he known the business world better or had some experience with industrial assembly lines, it is quite certain that he would have chosen different examples to illustrate his scorn. Farms, farmers, and farming, however, were at hand. Concord farmers, Yankees all, were as industrious (and proud of their industry) as Thoreau was idle (and defiant about his idleness). They would dig while he would lazily fish, their mutual distrust being quite apparent:

The farmer is wont to look with scorn and pride on a man sitting in a motionless boat a whole half day, but he does not realize that the object of his own labor is perhaps to add another dollar to his heap, nor through what coarsenesss and inhumanity to his family and servants he often accomplishes this.[40]

Here, thought Thoreau, is a fair sample of "dead unkind," well exemplifying foolishness, imbalance, and false values. For "the farmer is endeavoring to solve the problem of a livelihood by a formula more complicated than the problem itself. To get his shoestrings he speculates in herds of cattle."[41] (That he misses out on the fishing goes without saying!) Finally, in Thoreau's formula, as a man lives, so will he work (or not work because he wishes to live); but how farmers work is sharply reflected in their pattern of life:

> A model farm! where the house stands like a fungus in a muck-heap, chambers for men, horses, oxen, and swine, cleansed and uncleansed, all contiguous to one another! . . . A great grease-spot, redolent of manures and buttermilk.[42]

Farmers, of course, live close to nature and so are better off, in life and morality, for being removed (however wrongly motivated) from artificial civilization. But even they are guilty of yet another way of defiling human existence: that of misreading the intentions of nature and of misusing her gifts. "It appears to be a law," said Thoreau, "that you cannot have deep sympathy with both man and nature. Those qualities which bring you near to the one estrange you from the other."[43] And yet most men, farmers included, in their preference for human sympathy attempt to force man's ways on nature's ways. The streak of doubt in their personalities, for example, causes them to specialize only in "insects injurious to vegetation," thus manifesting a savage instinct to worship evil and to disavow the good of creation: "Though God may have pronounced his work good, we ask, 'Is it not poisonous?'"[44] Or take the case of the man who cuts down a white pine lot. Nature's way is immediately to sow oak thereon, man's way to burn the oak seedlings so that he may plant rye. And so, Thoreau comments, "he trifles with nature. I am chagrined for him." His "greediness defeats its own ends."[45] Then there are one's neighbors who shoot hawks in order to save their chickens. True, they are practicing a kind of economy, but it is not nature's economy. Rather it is "narrow and groveling. It is unnecessary to sacrifice the greater value to the less. I would rather never taste chickens' meat nor hens' eggs than never to see a hawk sailing through the upper air again."[46]

Nature's way is the way of the wild, and men defile their lives when they do not abide by this basic law of existence. A "tamed and, as it were, emasculated country" which can only result in a "maimed and imperfect nature" is the terrible penalty for breaking this law.[47] What is perhaps even worse, this violation is done in the name of civilization, so that every advance is really a retrogression, every stand for "progress" is done at the sacrifice of freedom and spontaneity. Man is less of a man, life is less lively, and humankind is doomed to be "the dead unkind" in every instance of man's law encroaching upon nature's law:

> The Anglo-American can indeed cut down and grub up all this waving forest, and make a stump speech, and vote for Buchanan on its ruins, but he cannot converse with the spirit of the tree he fells, he cannot read the poetry and mythology which retire as he advances.[48]

Civilized man is indeed ingenious at devising ways of contravening the purposes of nature and thus of impairing (in the sense of narrowing or rendering mean) his human existence. The last way which Thoreau identifies is most typical, very deadly. It is "the dead unkind's" refusal to subscribe to the laws which transcend all nature (human and otherwise), which underlie existence itself, and which are the life of life. These laws are spiritual, and to violate them can only result in a confirmation of meanness, a conviction of death.

To violate them is to sin, with sin understood not "in overt acts" but "in proportion to the time which has come behind us and displaced eternity,—that degree to which our elements are mixed with the elements of the world."[49] It is the sin of a civilized man, he who (unlike the primitive or the mystic) does not sojourn in nature, no longer "camps as for a night" but has "settled down on earth and forgotten heaven."[50] Such a sinner, in the name of civilization, "identifies himself with earth or the material. . . . Spirit is strange to him; he is afraid of ghosts."[51] Despite the fact that "men's bowels are far more slimy than their brains,"[52] they hug the earth and the matter of earth, living by their bodies only, failing to appreciate the beautiful and noble which transcend earth, distrusting their capacity for the ideal and their faculty for pure thought, and—what is more—refusing to tolerate in their mean presences those who would declare to them their higher calling. But, Thoreau warned, "Woe be to the generation that lets any higher faculty in its midst go unemployed! That is to deny God and know him not."[53] Woe, too, to that "people who have fallen far behind the significance of their symbols," and thus have lost "the sentiment of reverence." Called to a higher life, they "bethink [themselves] even as oxen."[54]

Surveying, then, the defilement of life which was the sole contribution of the "dead unkind" to civilization; pointing the finger at all civilized men hold dear as he held cheap—their crowds, their cities, their institutions, their commercial spirit; observing their "lawlessness" and materiality—Thoreau assumed the role of prophet in condemning the infidels. As Joel or Jeremias, he told them to "take a step forward and invent a new style of outhouse. Invent a salt that will save you and defend our nostrils." Calling them "stupid and timid chattels" and "clods of the valley," he had small hope of reaching all of them—"but I would fain arouse them by any stimulus to an intelligent life."[55]

Beginning as a prophet, he ultimately decided on the

stimulus of poetry, his trade in idleness. Most men want genius (it is why they are miserable), and a poet is a type of genius. Indeed, "no hawk that soars . . . is wilder than genius, and none is more persecuted or above persecution."[56] It is the genius of the poet, taking up where the prophet has left off, to point out the meaning of life to "the dead unkind." Such as these know no ideal, resting on the actual alone, "a sort of vomit in which the unclean love to wallow."[57] But the poet will put forth a life of the imagination. Such as these are practical, analytical. To them a bird is not a bird, and certainly not a promise of joy, but a "mote in the eye."[58] The poet will renew all things for them and thus restore their vision. Such as these have forgotten how to live. Thus their lives "affect me like opening of the tombs."[59] The poet will urge upon them his own vitality.

The trouble is that poets, the last hope of "the dead unkind," are themselves subject to the same ailments by which mankind sickens his world. For one thing, poets may both deceive and be deceived:

When the poetic frenzy seizes us, we run and scratch with our pen, delighting like cock, in the dust we make, but do not detect where the jewel lies, which perhaps we have in the meantime cast to a distance, or quite covered up again.[60]

For another, poets (out of disenchantment or disgust) may retire into a private existence, which is idyllic for themselves but useless to mankind:

Alas, the poet too is in one sense a sort of dormouse, gone into winter quarters of deep and serene thoughts, insensible to surrounding circumstances; his words are the relation of his oldest, finest memory, a wisdom drawn from the remotest existence. Other men lead a starved existence, meanwhile, like hawks that would fain keep on the wing, and trust to pick up a sparrow now and then.[61]

"A sparrow now and then" may not be enough to satisfy a starving man. But if both prophecies and poetry fail him, to whom shall he turn if he is to be revived?

Some say to one's friends, to the society of neighbors. Others say to the state, which is the society of the best hope of all. Thoreau says, as we shall see, that either remedy is worse than the sickness. In fact, men's reliance on such remedies is a major cause of the sickness, an excuse for defiling their world.

Chapter 5

SOCIETY AS BURDEN:
"UNREAL, INCREDIBLE, INSIGNIFICANT"

No fields are so barren to me as the men of whom I expect everything but get nothing.[1]

O such thin skins, such crockery, as I have to deal with! They are puffballs filled with dust and ashes.[2]

It seems odd that a man who was (quantitatively) friendless should have been intently, intensively concerned (qualitatively) about friendship. It is odder still that a social outlaw and political pariah would have troubled himself about the nature of government. Yet, as many passages in his journal will attest to the first oddity and some of his more notorious essays to the second, Thoreau was obviously very much taken with these subjects, or at least haunted by their grisly specter.

One supposes that he could have done without friends, that in fact he did get along with very few of them. What is more, having literally as well as figuratively separated himself from any union which happened along his solitary, self-demanding, limited, and delimiting way—a union with Concord, or the Commonwealth of Massachusetts, or America as a nation—it is quite clear that he could have done without any country whatsoever, save that of the countryside or one of his own fashioning. Nevertheless, he apparently thought it necessary to use experiences with friends and governments for teaching purposes. Object lessons could be made of them, or of the (to him) mystifying reliance that most men put upon them. Again, he knew that it was possible for him personally to manage his life very well unburdened by social and political relationships. But few of his fellows would even make the attempt at such management. They had to be apprised of the fact that taking up relationships meant, had to mean, the assumption of a burden, the burden of society. As he viewed the matter, this burden constituted a threat to the self and a possible negation of the self's purposes in life. In short, this burden—so necessary to men, so needless to Thoreau—was the second major impairment of meaningful human existence. To declare it so was his reason for evidencing such a concern about the topic.

An early journal entry, headed "scraps from a lecture on Society, written March 14, 1838, delivered before our Lyceum, April 11,"[3] suggests to us the connection between friendship and government in man's desire for society. It also suggests Thoreau's justification for regarding society as man's burden rather than as man's achievement.

He begins with the gravamen of his charge: the proverb, "Man was made for society," perhaps an original truth, has been converted into a lie, at the least into the contradiction of another truth—that society was made for man. Which takes priority? The answer is that inasmuch as man was not born into society, he—man—should take priority. The fact is, however, that he has been forced to yield to social organization. What is worse, it would appear that he freely yields.

This situation is most unfortunate, Thoreau claims. A man's *raison d'être* is within himself, else there is no justification of his existence. He is, or should be, a world unto himself. In fact, "the world that he is hides for a time [much too short a time, Thoreau believed] the world that he inhabits." Moreover, the essence of a man is a "profound secret," which no society can get at but which all society would obliterate if it could. Man should realize, from the depths of his own secret, that whatever he may hope to gain cannot be gained; for that which the individual wants to know about another individual is precisely that which he hides about himself.

Society is harmful as well as fraudulent. Alone, man loves his world, the source of his being. In society he hurts the earth, leaving it (hence also himself as the son of earth) wounded and scarred. Alone, he aspires to better things, whereas society always tends to level down. Alone, he is destined to discover the meaning of his individuality. In society (Thoreau offers cattle shows and college commencements as his examples of this point) he must lose his identity. Alone, he possesses a society which is complete, open, generous. In society, on the other hand,

> . . . you are getting all the while further and further from true society. Your silence was an approach to it, but your conversation is only a refuge from the encounter of men.[4]

Alone, man can tell the difference between the true and the false, the ideal and the illusion. In society he gives up his discrimination, looking always for nectar, locating only "short gingerbread."

The nature of society and the nature of man alone are at odds and must remain so: this is Thoreau's warning, no matter what the mutual attraction of the two natures seems to be. If so, then each must treat the other warily. Paradox will best explain the treatment. For example, once knock on your neighbor's door and you will soon determine that he is not in. Do not knock, however, and you will find him at home. To seek is not to find, to knock is not to enter. The reason is that, given the natures of both society and man, "utmost nearness," presumably the idea and ideal of socializing, may never be achieved by external, mechanical actions. Therefore, Thoreau concludes, let your seeing, hearing, and touching of your neighbor be an ideal only, his response felt merely. Should he require more of you (that is, paradoxically, less), then give him what he deserves of you:

> If thy neighbor hail thee to inquire how goes the world, feel thyself put to thy trumps to return a true and explicit answer. Plant the feet firmly, and, "will he nill he," dole out to him with strict and conscientious impartiality his modicum of a response.[5]

Society, which has been seen to hurt a man and deceive a man, can also cheapen a man. It demands too much of him in demanding not enough of him. It can never be his equal, although it sets itself up as his superior. It is so common, so casual, that it coarsens on contact. Beware and be advised, then: "Let not society be the element in which you swim." Imagine, rather, that you are a strip of land jutting into the sea, your lowest part (society's portion) constantly washed (and therefore of no particular consequence), your summit approached and reached only occasionally.

Thoreau's argument may be reduced to a few simple propositions: that society has no value in itself; that the individual may gain little from it but stand to lose much because of it; that the notion of a man fulfilling himself in society is a snare and a delusion; and that what society itself has proposed as its chief use to man—its relief of his burden of solitude—actually imposes a far heavier burden on him, all the more difficult to bear (that is, to tolerate) because it is "unreal, incredible, and insignificant."[6]

But man, brainwashed by society, has tended not to accept these propositions. Therefore he does in fact bear the "unreal, incredible, and insignificant" burden of society. Thoreau's task is to define the burden for man in the two most typical forms man has given it: the society of friends and the society of states.

The Society of Friends

Thoreau's fundamental view of friendship, not unexpectedly, is peacefully based but martially expressed. He sees it as "the fruit which the year should bear," something (a distinctly and distinctively pastoral something) well beyond the "ordinary courtesy and intercourse of men."[7] It begins in the joy of "two or more individuals who from constitution sympathize." However, the joy of neither may be sacrificed to that of the other. That "my heat is latent to you" should give pleasure to both parties; nevertheless, because "I am under the awful necessity to be what I am," as presumably the other is to be what he is, joy will be lost, as will be friendship, if it is not possible to transcend the need for excuses, apologies, and embarrassing explanations which joyful individuals are above but which mutual associations seem to require.[8] Friendship is its own excuse for being and cannot be "made," in the ordinary sense of the term, because it "is not his to give nor mine to receive."[9] Finally, although a friendship may derive from some defect in a man, it is its nature, by supplying the defect, to render itself unnecessary:

> I hate that my motive for visiting a friend should be that I want society; that it should be in my poverty and weakness, and not in his and my riches and strength. His friendship should make me strong enough to do without him.[10]

On the other hand, Thoreau has a way of mixing his metaphors when discussing the general nature of friends and friendship, relying rather heavily on figures of war to illustrate his points. For example, it is with some uneasiness that he declares "the price of friendship [to be] the total surrender of yourself."[11] He will speak of a visit to a friend in terms of walking "amid the columns of a ruined temple," as if a recent carnage had devastated the land. Indeed, it did—but only "enemies publish themselves" whereas "the friend never declares his love."[12]

Most striking and only semiparadoxical, moreover, is Thoreau's repeated reference to the friend as foe, to friendship as a state of war. Thus "we have nothing to fear from our foes; God keeps a standing army for that service; but we have no ally against our Friends, those ruthless vandals."[13] Thus, also, "I cannot pardon my enemy; let him pardon himself."[14]

Similarly, his references to friends (that is, to the demands he would put upon them) seem to be expressed somewhat ambiguously—just possibly because of ambivalence. He seems, on the one hand, to be reasonable enough in what he asks. On the other hand, we can detect a mocking tone which would seem to indicate that no friend he has yet met could come up to his standards. "I demand of my companion some evidence that he has traveled further than the sources of the Nile," he said, "that he has seen something, that he has been out of town, out of the house."[15] Such a request sounds reasonably direct—until some would-be friend should have to interpret and apply it. By the same token, what he asks of his host at dinner is more easily savored as a figure of speech than translated into a course of action likely to please him:

> If my friend would take a quarter part the pains to show me himself that he does to show me a piece of roast beef, I should feel myself irresistibly invited. . . . I find the beef hot and well done, but him rare.[16]

How, it may be asked, can the friend "show" himself "well done" without at the same time exhibiting a rigid, fixed quality, so unyielding as not to admit of Thoreau's ministrations, but at the same time suggesting a set position to which Thoreau is beckoned against his will? How, to put this another way, may a man have seriousness and depth enough to escape the accusation of "unreal, incredible, and insignificant" and still leave Thoreau feeling, as he said he felt with Alcott, unconfined and unrestrained: "He has no creed. He is not pledged to any institution. The sanest man I ever knew"?[17] Indeed, is there nothing to the idea of a "most profitable" friend than that he be an outdoor type, or is Thoreau simply exaggerating because he knows that his real demands cannot be met? His question is direct enough: "Who is the most profitable companion? He who has been picking cranberries and chopping wood, or he who has been attending the opera all his days?"[18] The answer, to anyone else but Thoreau, cannot be so simple.

The social institution of friendship, then, as well as friends in fact, Thoreau treated rather skeptically. Whether his skepticism in the matter was a cause or effect of his leaning toward the ideal cannot really be determined. But it was definitely his tendency. In discussing the reason why friends repelled him while nature attracted him, he stated the point exactly: "Yet, strictly speaking, the same must be true of nature and of man; our ideal is the only real. It is not the finite and temporal that satisfies or concerns us in either case."[19] Therefore, in choosing a single companion he would wish to translate the transcendental notion of manhood into a criterion: "I would not forget that I deal with infinite and divine qualities in my fellow. . . . Even the tired laborers I meet on the road, I really meet as traveling gods."[20]

Sometimes this divine quality will be immediately apparent, suggesting out of itself a reason for friendship, as when one comes in "contact with a pure, uncompromising spirit, that is somewhere wandering in the atmosphere" and that takes the form of virtue or moral "loveliness."[21] Although friendship, like beauty and virtue, is what it is,[22] divine in its ontological integrity, Thoreau found a use in a friend—the emulation of his nobility. Two interesting passages present this use quite succinctly:

> I hear no good news but ever some trait of a noble character. It reproaches me plaintively. I am mean in contrast, but again am thrilled and elevated that I can see my own meanness, and again still, that my own aspiration is realized in that other.[23]

> Then first I conceive of a true friendship, when some rare specimen of manhood presents itself. It seems

the mission of such to commend virtue to mankind, but by their own carriage and conduct. We may then worship moral beauty without the formality of a religion.[24]

The friendship proposed by such a one is indeed a kind of religion. Thoreau called it "the highest sympathy," as "far from pity as from contempt," the "charity [of which] is generosity, its virtue nobleness."[25] All that is required for membership in this cult is one person seeking nobility in another, forming thereby a "community of one" in a "pledge of holy living."[26] All? Yes, but it is not so readily attainable precisely because it is an ideal and always just a little bit beyond one's grasp:

The nearest approach to a community of love in these days is like the distant breaking of waves on the seashore. An ocean there must be, for it washes our beach. This alone do all men sail for, trade for, plow for, fight for.[27]

In the ideal this community (or society) of love which a friend holds out to us has certain marks by which it may be recognized, rules by which it must abide. First, it is not what vulgar men make of it or think it is—"not so kind as is imagined; it has not much human blood in it but consists with a certain disregard for men and their erections, the Christian duties and humanities, while it purifies the air like electricity."[28] Second, it may not be cheapened or coarsened by the usual amenities. The reason is that "the more complete our sympathy, the more our senses are struck dumb, and we are repressed by a delicate respect, so that to indifferent eyes we are least his friend, because no vulgar symbols pass between us."[29] Third, its strategies and stratagems ("a war of positions, of silent tactics") are explicit in what shall be allowed, what denied. For example, "friends do not interchange their common wealth, but each puts his finger into the private coffer of the other." Or, "A friend does not afford us cheap contrasts and encounters. He forbears to ask explanations, but doubts and surmises with full faith, as we silently ponder our fates." Or, "My friend is not chiefly wise or beautiful or noble. At least it is not for me to know it."[30] Last, true friendship, if it be really true, is beyond analysis and discussion. Presumably, therefore, if it must be examined, it does not exist. For "all that can be said of Friendship is like Botany to flowers. How can the understanding take account of its friendliness?"[31]

Now with the ideal of friendship set so high in Thoreau's mind, it is little wonder that he was constantly meeting with something considerably less than the ideal; that is, with the "unreal, incredible, and insignificant." When he complains, however, he must not be thought unreasonable or unjust. The society of friends as he idealized it is no burden, but man has frequently settled for a society which is a burden but which he still takes for an ideal. So Thoreau's first design is not so much to differentiate between the two societies as to criticize man for not habitually making the differentiation. His second design, then, is to identify all that was wrong with the society of man's invention, to declare out of his own experience the burden of incompletely realized friendships, of false friends.

As in other matters, he is willing to take part of the blame on himself. As he put it, "If I have not succeeded in my friendships, it was because I demanded more of them and did not put up with what I could get; and I got no more partly because I gave so little."[32] Or if it should turn out that "no fields are so barren to me as the men of whom I expect everything but get nothing,"[33] the reason is "as much by my own ill treatment and ill valuing of them, profaning of them, cheapening of them, as by their cheapening of themselves."[34] The basic trouble may be something innately, integrally natural to friendship: "If there is any one with whom we have a quarrel, it is most likely that that one makes some just demand on us which we disappoint."[35] Or it may stem from a simple misunderstanding: "He finds fault with me that I walk alone, when I pine for want of a companion."[36] Or it may be that he is crotchety because he is so very jealous of his own individuality and resentful of in-

trusions upon it: "Talked, or tried to talk, with R. W. E.
Lost my time—nay, almost my identity."[37] However he
explained it, Thoreau would not seek to evade his share
of the blame.

But he seemed to feel that the fault lay primarily with
friendship itself, or at least with his particular friends.
And it is this fault that he would disclose because it is
this that makes the society of friends burdensome. Each
and all of his complaints, then, begin in a subjective state,
and point toward an objectively moral lesson.

"I love my friends very much," he said, "but I find
that it is no use to go see them. I hate them commonly
when I am near them. They belie themselves and deny
me continually."[38] The point is that a friendship becomes
burdensome if it does not improve the persons of friends.
Again, "My friends, my friends, it does not cheer me to
see them. They but express their want of faith in me or
in mankind."[39] The point here is that friendship, which
should be based on trust, more often than not is founded
on weakness and maintained by deceit. Or, in a more
characteristic choice of language, Thoreau bewailed his
lot in this fashion: "O such thin skins, such crockery,
as I have to deal with! . . . They are puffballs filled with
dust and ashes."[40] These are harsh, misanthropic terms
if taken personally, but their point is that, whereas friendships ought to be substantial and satisfying, they have a
way of becoming insufficient ("unreal, incredible, and
insignificant") and unlovely.

What do friends do wrong? For one thing, they turn
something simple into something burdensomely complex
—as when they "begin to deal in confessions, break silence, make a theme of friendship . . . and descend to
merely human relations!"[41] For another, the manners or
customs that they seem to think essential to friendship
frequently separate rather than unify the parties. Thus
"between me and my friend what unfathomable distance.
All mankind, like motes and insects, are between us."
Putting this another way at another time, Thoreau said:
"You cheat me, you keep me at a distance with your
manners. I know of no other dishonesty, no other devil."

For these reasons, he says, friendships do not cease; they decay.[42] For a third thing, even the finest of friends seem shallow. They are "not serene, a world in themselves," but are guilty of "an immense frivolity. They do not teach me the lessons of honesty and sincerity that the brute beasts do."[43] Fourth, they tend to be selfish, requiring "sympathy themselves rather than are able to render it to others. They want faith and mistake their private ail for an infected atmosphere."[44] Last and most significant, despite the fact that it is the very nature of friendship to understand and to trust, friends are usually the first not to understand and not to trust. And so, despairing of a meaningful relationship but unwilling to take on the burden of a senseless one, Thoreau was finally forced to retreat into a private world where "like cuttlefish we conceal ourselves."[45]

Here, at least and at last, he could take his stand, unburdened even if quite alone. Here he could be free of that worry and doubt which beclouded even the closest of his friendships and which constituted (he thought) a threat to all friendship: the concern that somehow friends would cut him off from nature. As he put it, "I am sure that if I call for a companion on my walk I have relinquished in my design some closeness of communion with Nature."[46] Nor would he be troubled that "if I am too cold for human friendship . . . I shall not soon be too cold for natural influences,"[47] for it is man, not nature, who estranges man from man and man from nature.

True, he takes leave of society—and with it the burden of society—not without some regret:

What if we feel a yearning to which no breast answers? I walk alone. My heart is full. Feelings impede the current of my thought. I knock on the earth for my friend. I expect to meet him at every turn; but no friend appears, and perhaps none is dreaming of me. I am tired of frivolous society. . . .[48]

Nevertheless, regretful or not, he made his move, ultimately confident that he would gain more than he had given up—and urging upon all those burdened by the "unreal, incredible, and insignificant" a similar confidence: "But special I remember thee, Wachusett, who like me, standest alone without society."[49]

The Society of States

If in Thoreau's judgment friendships were to be regarded as burdensome to an individual because they are unnecessary, restrictive, and unrewarding, it followed quite logically in his thought that states, simply more organized societies of friends, had even less of a reason for being, were yet more confining, and yielded virtually nothing at all to man's natural or spiritual improvement. Since a state is an extension or multiplication of the relationships proposed by friendships, all the defects of the latter's lower-level, relatively simple affinities would be magnified by the former's higher-level, obviously complex demands. Moreover, although human experience can turn up instances of friendlessness and even whole lifetimes of comparative solitude, hardly anyone ever heard of a stateless person or would think it possible to live without some ministration of government. This being the case, Thoreau's task of condemning the burden of man's attraction to the society of the state was a particularly difficult one, certainly not a popular one.

In a sense, it may be said that he went about this task using a method exactly opposite to Plato's in *The Republic*. Whereas that classic used the analogy of the state to instruct in the psychology of individuals, that is to say a larger form to disclose the secrets of the smaller, Thoreau's treatment of friends is a meticulously precise analysis in miniature of his theories about statehood and statecraft. He wrote and thought less about government than about friendship because the subject touched him less, striking him as virtually irrelevant to his purposes in life or way of life. Nor did he himself ever pretend to be an authority on political economy. Nevertheless, a fair portion of his work was given over to the society of the state as a burden: the state in general, the American state in particular.

[79]

In general his attitude was succinctly summarized as follows: "To one who habitually endeavors to contemplate the true state of things, the political state can hardly be said to have any existence whatever. It is unreal, incredible, and insignificant to him."[50] There are two reasons underlying this attitude. One is that, as far as he is concerned, there is no room in life for government. As he said, "I have other affairs to attend to. I came into this world, not chiefly to make this a good place to live in, but to live in it. . . ."[51] Thus it is that a government seems unreal to him. The other reason is that even the best of governments at their best appeal to a part of his nature which is absolutely closed to such an appeal—that is, the appeal to his social instinct. The man who wants a government, he claimed, "has dwindled into an Odd Fellow —one who may be known by the development of his organ of gregariousness, and a manifest lack of intellect and self-reliance." What is perhaps worse, such socializing, even in the "name of Order and Civil Government," forces us "to pay homage to and support our own meanness."[52] Thus it is that a government seems incredible (that is, how can it be taken seriously?) and insignificant (without relevance) to him.

Now occasionally, if only indirectly, Thoreau would seem to concede the possibility of government having a use and purpose. He said that "the effect of a good government is to make life more valuable" and that "the only government I recognize is that power that establishes justice in the land." But he finished off both these remarks in such a negative way as to suggest that, more usually, governments make life less valuable and tend to establish injustice in the land.[53]

Moreover, his indictment of government in general can be both specific and severe. States, for example, promote (are only good for promoting) war as a way of life. Calling war a madness, he wonders "what asylum is there for nations to go to?"[54] States are so self-serving —and demanding in their service—that no man can maintain his freedom and dignity in their service. "It is impossible," he said, "to give the soldier a good education without making him a deserter. His natural foe is the government that drills him."[55] States, by definition and customary practice, are opposed to the natural way of life, to nature herself, "legislating chiefly for oxen," rarely for natural resources by which they are sustained.[56] Even when most vigorous and supposedly flourishing, they are seen to "exist and batten on another moldering one" rather than having a life of their own.[57] Finally, states (or those who run them) interfere with a man's natural way of life. Thus "the remembrance of the baseness of politicians spoils my walks. My thoughts are murder to the State; I endeavor in vain to observe Nature; my thoughts involuntarily go plotting against the State. I trust that all just men will conspire."[58]

So apprised of the condition of states set off against the needs of the individual, Thoreau advises the citizen to take the next logical step: to secede. He even offered a model declaration of independence: "Know all men by these presents, that I, Henry Thoreau, do not wish to be regarded as a member of any incorporated society which I have not joined."[59] Why should he, or any man, accept membership in a society that was "half-witted, . . . timid as a lone woman with her silver spoons, . . . and did not know its friends from its foes . . ."?[60] Why, indeed, voluntarily delimit oneself and thus commit suicide? For "if a plant cannot live according to its nature, it dies; and so a man."[61]

There, in a phrase, is the thrust of his argument against all government: it runs contrary to a man's nature. "I do not wish to quarrel with any man or nation," he said. "I do not wish to split hairs, to make fine distinctions, or set myself up as better than any neighbors."[62] But if government derives from the consent of the governed, and this consent be withheld *according to a man's nature,* then to submit to government is indeed "unreal" and "incredible." And if that government be a bad one, then the submission takes on a terrible significance.

The American government in particular Thoreau found bad for a variety of reasons. On the local level it was responsible for nonsense like a poll-tax. On the state level

Thoreau spoke of it as "moral fungus" and "consolidated deviltry" because it sided with the immoral (lotteries, for example) rather than with the moral.[63] On the national level it sinned grievously. Slavery was the sin.

"As I love my life," Thoreau said, "I would side with the light."[64] That light disclosed "a state covered with disgrace,"[65] one run by "stupid and timid chattels, pretending to read history and our Bibles but desecrating every house and every day we breathe in," one which was supposed to be "representative"—but "what a monster of a government [is it] where the noblest faculties of the mind, and the whole heart, are not represented?"[66] It discloses, to free men in the land of the free, a terrible slavery and servility—"a decaying and a death offensive to all healthy nostrils. We do not complain that they live, but that they do not get buried."[67] At one time America was free—and alive—a state where "you were at liberty to pursue such a life as may ennoble you."[68] Now it has become "an audacious government" taking a step "toward its own dissolution."[69]

Having become a burden, it should be cast off, Thoreau believed. "It is not an era of repose. We have used up all our inherited freedom. If we would save our lives, we must fight for them."[70] It is the time for revolt, because "if private men are obliged to perform the offices of government, to protect the weak and dispense justice, then the government becomes only a hired man."[71] It is time for treason, because resistance to "tyranny here below has its origin in, and is first committed by, the power which makes and forever re-creates man."[72]

In general, then, governments restrict a man. Bad governments degrade him. But man's first duty is to himself, to be a free self and not merely a citizen. Therefore, Thoreau concluded, "I would remind my countrymen that they are to be men first, and Americans only at a late and convenient hour."[73] So much for the burden of the state.

Society, indeed, is man's burden. It promises him, through the society of friends, the completion of his solitary nature. Ultimately, it would destroy that nature. It promises him, through the society of states, a civil order and civil liberty for his life. In fact, it reduces his well-ordered existence to chaos and condemns him to penal servitude.

Thoreau never says that a man must do without friends, that all governments are to be abolished forthwith. He does say that the essence of societal relationships runs counter to the essence of the self. Insofar as it does, then society overwhelms a man and breaks his back—and spirit. It does it with a burden: unreal because it is unnecessary; incredible because it may not be sustained without impunity; and insignificant because it offers meaningless blandishments in exchange for ideal value.

The man of purpose, he who would fulfill the self, must know in which ways he has defiled his existence, the nature of the burdens he bears. He should also know—and be prepared to confront—certain other evils in his life. For these he is not responsible, although he must suffer them as if he were. How to confront them, how to suffer them, how to translate them: these things Thoreau would treat next.

Chapter 6

CONFRONTATION WITH EVIL: "CHAOS AND OLD NIGHT"

Is not disease the rule of existence?[1]

It smelled like a dead rat in the ceiling. Pray, what was Nature thinking of when she made this? She almost puts herself on a level with those who draw in privies.[2]

We speak of an "unprincipled" man in a double sense: as one who is evil because no law higher than himself or spiritual light other than his own darkness of soul directs his actions, and as one who does evil because his criterion of conduct is beneath that established or accepted by the gods, by other men, or by goodness itself. Both senses depend upon and derive from our conviction of an objectively existing code or concept, the nobility of which is beyond proof or the need of proving. There must be such a thing, or else virtue can be neither known nor practiced. There must be such a thing, or else morality will disappear from the face of the earth, and with it the possibility of living a good or at least an ordered existence. In a word, we admit to principle when we take note of nonprinciple.

Thoreau spent a lifetime looking for, living by, and instructing in this principle. Curiously, however, his best expression and summary judgment of just what it is were cast in negative terms—as if he had concluded that we may know the day only by night, the good through evil. What is more, he seemed to assert that that principle, whatever we may take it to be, must reckon with its opposite. Unlike most men, then, he admits to nonprinciple whenever he takes note of principle. His thoughts are ultimately happy, but they are grounded in sadness. He proclaimed the good life, but he plainly, painfully detected evil in the world. Mostly he was serene, but he saw and he said the multitudinous ways in which men suffer and the universe agonizes. Therefore, any substantial account of him should seriously estimate the role that evil played in the drama of his being. Therefore, too, a proper, rounded understanding of his positive philosophy should proceed from his message of negation.

The account and the understanding can begin with a discussion of one of his last prose pieces, all the more poignant and perhaps consequential because it was conceived in pain, written in the shadow of death, and (published posthumously) put forth from his grave. Not without significance is it called "Life Without Principle."[3]

He opens with a complaint and a promise, both of which immediately suggest that he is about serious business. The complaint has to do with the lecturer (or writ-

er, for that matter) who talks "not in or near to his heart
... but toward his extremities and superficies." The promise is that he will speak from his soul, hurting the hearer,
to be sure, but to a good purpose and for a good reason:
"As the time is short, I will leave out all the flattery and
retain all the criticism."

Initially, this criticism is directed against work and
commerce. Business is trivial, a time-wasting enterprise, he
says—and there is very little time. A man should choose
an occupation which yields him "real profit," which (to
Thoreau) means little money. One reason for this is that
"the ways by which you may get money almost without
exception lead downward." A more important reason is
that "the aim of the laborer should be, not to get a living
... but to perform well a certain work." Living is "invit-
ing and glorious," getting a living interferes with life. Indeed, he was persuaded that "cold and hunger seem more
friendly to my nature than those methods which men have
adopted or devised to ward them off." Some, of course,
are born rich and therefore need not work for their
living. Theirs is another risk: "Merely to come into the
world the heir of a fortune is not to be born, but to be
still-born." Finally, there are those who neither work nor
live off their inheritance but who try to maintain themselves by luck and speculation (gold-seekers or stock-
brokers, for example). For them Thoreau has nothing
but scorn:

> I know of no more startling development of the im-
> morality of trade, and all the common modes of get-
> ting a living. The philosophy and poetry and religion
> of such a mankind are not worth the dust of a
> puffball. The hog that gets his living by rooting . . .
> would be ashamed of such company.[4]

Having disposed of the fortune hunters who bring their
special form of decay into this world, Thoreau goes on to
certain other decadents: the preachers (so few "moral
teachers" among them, he points out) through whose
ministries "the spirit of sect and bigotry has planted its

hoof among the stars"; all those who crowd their lives with things that are "infra-human, a kind of vegetation" —things like newspapers, politics, gossip ("When our life ceases to be inward and private, conversation degenerates into mere gossip"), manners ("Conventionalities are at length as bad as impurities"), and narrow, narrowing routines ("We are provincial because we do not find at home our standards, because we do not worship truth but the reflection of truth"); and that class of men who, hurried, harassed, and antagonistic, treats life as if it were a race or a contest: "Pray, let us live without being drawn by dogs, Esquimaux-fashion, tearing over hill and dale, and biting each other's ears."

All, out of ignorance or smallness, bring a kind of evil to human existence, doing it and themselves injury because they live without principle. But in fortune's good time this kind of evil will both reveal and shame itself, as "murder will out." In time "mankind will hang itself on a tree." When this happens, then the saving remnant can get back to what is really important, after attending the last rites of their foolish brothers: "You come from attending the funeral of mankind to attend to a natural phenomenon. A little thought is sexton to all the world."

The determination of just which "little thought" is Thoreau's central theme in "Life Without Principle." The real life without principle is not simply a matter of men who are unprincipled. Their evil is venial only, the worst feature of it being that it blinds them to the terrible and terrifying mortal sins of life itself. To put this another way, man's depredations are real and disturbing but they are also explicable. Pain, sickness, death, mortal sorrow, and the destructive forces within nature, on the other hand, are more terrible and less easily explained. To be sure, moral evil is to be condemned. But who or what is responsible for physical evil? Is there abroad a principle of nonprinciple? Moreover, although moral theologians may teach that physical evil comes about as a result of moral evil, Thoreau seems to feel that a full confrontation with the former will help men eradicate the latter, perhaps because the physical is a type of the moral, at

least because coming to grips with what you can do nothing about is a sure, realistic preparation for what you can
manage on your own.

Thoreau's "little thought," then, proposes three points
for meditation. One, "God did not make the world in
jest." His meaning here is that the awful solemnity of living is no more to be discounted by a thoughtless, frivolous
existence than by one in which the minor flaws of humanity obscure the major flaws in being itself. Two, "We
do not live for idle amusement. I would not run round a
corner to see the world blow up." Now his meaning is
that the best of life, a very serious business indeed, is
realized through a clear view of the worst. It would be as
foolish to forget this as it would be to pass our time in fun
and games, expecting unlimited joy and continuous amusement. So serious is it that not even a catastrophe on the
next block should distract us from the lurking terror on
our own. Three, despite (possibly because of) the grave
purposes of creation and the solemn embracing thereof,
Thoreau puts forth a disciplined, chastened, but ultimately hopeful attitude:

> Why should we not meet, not always as dyspeptics,
> to tell our bad dreams, but sometimes as eupeptics,
> to congratulate each other on the ever glorious morn-
> ing? I do not make an exorbitant demand, surely.[5]

This is to say that joy relates to our sadness. All that is
needful, once we have become convinced that existence is
worse than we had supposed, is to search within our
despondency for the proof that it is better than we had
imagined.

Now Thoreau, like any man, preferred states of joy
and affection to states of depression. He required of his
journal, that confidante of his inner life and expression of
his outer, that it "be the record of my love. I would write
in it only of the things I love, my affection for any aspect
of the world, what I love to think of."[6] But the harshness
of reality required candor of him, nothing less than the
bittersweetness of "unquestionable truth—though it were

the announcement of our dissolution."[7] How explain his
usual serenity? Doesn't truth exact tears of a man? To one
of his contemporaries who was puzzled by such questions
he responded thus:

> You ask if there is no doctrine of sorrow in my
> philosophy. Of acute sorrow I suppose that I know
> comparatively little. My saddest and most genuine
> sorrows are apt to be transient regrets. The place of
> sorrow is supplied, perchance, by a certain hard and
> proportionably barren indifference. I am of kin to
> the sod, and partake largely of its dull patience.[8]

This answer is true enough in its way. But it does
not go far enough in several respects. Thoreau did know
sorrow of many sorts; if it was not acute, the explanation
is not to be found in his indifference or dullness but in
his balance and proportion learned, along with patience,
from earth's patterns of compensation. Moreover, "transient regrets" is hardly the phrase to apply to his constant
consciousness of wounds: those he inflicted and those he
suffered. Such wounds were shadows of evil, such a consciousness was his wrestling with the problem of evil.

In his most morose moments he was apt to think that
all trouble, his and that of the world, derived from interior (and therefore untreatable) conditions, from the
atmosphere of the soul, one might say. Then he would
write that "the thought of what I am, of my pitiful conduct, deters me from receiving what joy I might from
the glorious days that visit me."[9] Or, extending this attitude
outward, he would exclaim, "How awful is the least unquestionable meanness, when we cannot deny that we
have been guilty of it. There seem to be no bounds to
our unworthiness."[10] And, if this mood seems to be indict-
ing what appear to be actual sins only, we should be reminded that he can speak doubts and recriminations much
more universal and fundamental: "When a shadow flits
across the landscape of the soul, where is the substance?
Has it always its origin in sin? and is that sin in me?"[11]
In short, differing quite sharply with typical transcen-

dental thought, he did believe in sin both original and actual, did brand sin evil, and did sorrow because of it.

For the most part, however, introspective moments to the contrary, we find Thoreau notified of the presence of evil and called to sorrow thereby through the more external but equally dark ministry of bodily pain and death.

His body was a two-edged sword to him. On the one hand, it was the instrument of his happiness, affording him joy when little else did. For example:

> One while we do not wonder that so many commit suicide, life is so barren and worthless; we only live on by an effort of the will. Suddenly our condition is ameliorated, and even the barking of a dog is a pleasure to us. So closely is our happiness bound up with our physical condition, and one reacts on the other.[12]

On the other hand, should anything go wrong with the body, both outlook and insight are affected. Thus:

> . . . in sickness all is deranged. I had yesterday a kink in my back and a general cold, and as usual it amounted to a cessation of life. I lost for the time my rapport or relation to nature. Sympathy with nature is an evidence of perfect health. You cannot perceive beauty but with a serene mind.[13]

Therefore, a little thing such as the loss of an abscessed tooth would reduce him to dirt: "I have felt cheap, and hardly dared hold up my head among men. . . . What a great matter a little spark kindleth!"[14] Putting this another way, he said: "How much of my well-being, think you, depends on the condition of my lung and stomach—such cheap pieces of nature."[15]

Well, then, he suffered from poor teeth, diseased lungs, and a weak stomach. Are these things evil? Not in themselves. What they do is to point to, call it, a principle of pain rooted in human existence. It is this which is evil— perhaps in its origin, certainly in the way in which it wars against joy and vitality. But a man like Thoreau could derive something from anything, could find uplifting lessons in everything. Did he not learn to translate his pain and, translating it, to transcend it? He did indeed. What he learned then became the substance of the epistle he addressed to anyone so joy-set, so unaware of the dark nature of being, that physical discomfort would leave him more bewildered than hurt. It is to say that "sickness should not be allowed to extend further than the body. As soon as I find my chest is not of tempered steel, and heart of adamant, I bid goodbye to these and look out a new nature."[16]

Similarly, although one might say that Thoreau was preoccupied with thoughts of death and dying, he managed to turn these thoughts, as those of sickness, into something less damning, if no less evil. Read one way, these thoughts seem as darkly fatalistic as any which may be found in primitive (Anglo-Saxon, for example) literature or pagan philosophy. The sight of old people suggested to him the finality of life, admitting no Christian hope ("O death, where is thy victory?") or Transcendentalist optimism: "How earthy old people become,—as moldy as the grave! Their wisdom smacks of the earth. There is no foretaste of immortality in it."[17] This being the case, Thoreau's view of life may be said to end at and be repressed by the grave. What is the life of a man? "He wanders round until his end draws nigh / And then lays down his aged head to lie / And this is life, that is that famous strife."[18] Moreover, man is foolish to wear himself out in trying to maintain his health as if thereby to cheat the grave or at least to postpone it— "as if consistency were the secret of health, while the poor inconsistent aspirant man, seeking to live a pure life, feeding on air, divided against himself, cannot stand, but pines and dies after a life of sickness. . . ."[19] It is surely an evil, then, life's built-in evil, to hope so much, to realize so little. And so it is, he tells us, that in the presence of death (particularly the death of loved ones) we stand unredeemed:

> I have touched a body which was flexible and warm,
> yet tenantless—and warmed by what fire? . . . I per-
> ceive that we partially die ourselves through sympathy
> at the death of each of our friends or near relatives.
> Each such experience is an assault on our vital
> force.[20]

Read another way, however, Thoreau's thoughts on
death, which is evil because it seems unredeemable and
pointless, unprincipled if you will, contain not so much a
note of consolation as of conviction, a conviction that
might also be called triumphal, even if it is naturally
rather than supernaturally based. He put forward the
human dignity of death which in part compensates for
its evil. For example, having observed a bit of human
bone and flesh on a deserted beach, he said:

> I was impressed as if there were an understanding
> between them and the ocean which necessarily left
> one out, with my sniveling sympathies. That dead
> body had taken possession of the shore, and reigned
> over it as no living one could, in the name of a cer-
> tain majesty which belonged to it.[21]

Moreover, the announcement of death, such as a funeral
bell solemnly tolling in harmony with nature's own stately
rhythms, tells us that "in proportion as death is more
earnest than life, it is better than life."[22] Death may be evil,
but at least it is not trivial.

It still remains for us to discover precisely in which ways
Thoreau's message of death ultimately pierces the mask
of its evil to reveal whatever good may be hidden there.
What we should notice is that, in the three possible approaches to death (death as an idea, the death of a friend,
and one's own death), Thoreau emphasized a single
point: the serious relationship between life and death.
For example, speculating in general on the topic, he
said: "The amount of it is, if a man is alive, there is
always danger that he may die, though the danger must
be allowed to be less in proportion as he is dead and

alive to begin with."[23] In other words, as a man lives, indeed as much as a man lives, so will he die. Fully to live is less completely, or devastatingly, to die. The same point is made in different words as he comments on the execution of Captain John Brown:

> This event advertises me that there is such a fact as death—the possibility of a man's dying. It seems as if no man had ever died in America; for in order to die, you must first have lived.[24]

Finally, even the thought of his own dying and death maintains this image of a full life negating the evil of death. As a young child, worrying about death but far from consoled by visions of an afterlife, he is reported to have said that he "did not want to go to heaven, because he could not carry his sled with him."[25] Thus the communion of saints does not make up for a good belly-whop, nor does the beatific vision do as much to take the blackness out of the grave as a romp in the snow. As a dying man (although still a young man) he made the same point: "I have not many months to live. I may add that I am enjoying existence as much as ever, and regret nothing."[26] And then there are his comments as reported by his sister Sophia, comments made in the last hours left to him. These, too, sustain the same gallantry, which turns out to be nothing more nor less than the satisfaction of having lived fully:

> He remarked to me that there was as much comfort in perfect disease as in perfect health, the mind always conforming to the condition of the body. The thought of death, he said, could not begin to trouble him. His thoughts had entertained him all his life, and did still.[27]

If these thoughts are not theological, neither are they philosophical. What looks like Stoicism in them is really something much more positive and life-affirming. He felt that you should no more be resigned to dying than to living but should derive the most from every moment of life, including the moment of death.

Death is an evil, an irrevocable evil, then, only if one's life has been wasted. Therefore, life itself makes death irrelevant. Living fully means to apply one's complete attention to its solemnities, for "we begin to die, not in our senses or extremities, but in our divine faculties. Our members may be sound, but our genius and imagination betray signs of decay."[28] Indeed, living solemnly, one can reduce all evil—and the terror of evil —to an absurdity:

The most serious events have their ludicrous aspect, such as death; but we cannot excuse ourselves when we have taken this view of them only. It is pardonable when we spurn the proprieties, even the sanctities, making them stepping stones to something higher.[29]

Now it happened that nature supplied Thoreau with most of these "stepping stones." But before they led to "something higher" they directed him through a Manichean world filled with disgusting sights, with brutal hostility, with disease and death. Not only was this natural world "red in tooth and claw" but also malignant and quite possibly malevolent. It was evil raw, evil real, evil basic to existence. This view of nature revealed "something savage and awful, though beautiful. This was that earth of which we have heard, made out of Chaos and Old Night."[30] A sight of this "vast, titanic, and inhuman" in nature put man "at disadvantage, caught him alone, and pilfers him of some of his divine faculty."[31] Such a sight, confronting him, must be confronted by him—because it proposes a fundamental question to him. "It is *the* question, to the exclusion of every other interest." Life, that is an understanding of and rule for life, depends on the answer.[32]

Beginning his quest for the answer, Thoreau observed the blight that seemed to be on the world: lily pads riddled by insects, galled trees, rotten vegetation, spoiled

fruit. "Is not disease the rule of existence?" he inquired.[33]
The response is an alarming but significant Yes. "Disease
is, in fact, the rule of our terrestrial life and the prophecy
of a celestial life. . . . Disease is not the accident of
the individual, nor even of the generation, but of life itself."[34] Only in the sense that misery loves company
could he extract any comfort from a response like that.
So he continued his search among the growing things:
one type of fungus "pushed out like a hernia";[35] another
type smelled "like a dead rat in the ceiling. Pray, what
was Nature thinking of when she made this? She
almost puts herself on a level with those who draw in
privies";[36] the "heart wood of the poison-dogwood" has
a "singular rotten, yellow look and a spiritous or apothe-
cary odor";[37] even the falling leaves from a tree make
"the whole earth . . . a cemetery . . . [where] there are
no lying or vain epitaphs."[38]

Turning next to animal life, Thoreau found more terror
—and also further points for meditation. The eel properly
disgusted him: "What a repulsive and gluttonous-looking
creature . . . made to plow the mud and wallow in filth,
with its slimy skin."[39] But at least the snapping turtle,
for all its ugliness, can teach something to humans, even
if what it teaches is not very pleasant: "The insensibility
and toughness of his infancy make our life, with its disease
and low-spirits, ridiculous. He impresses me as the rudi-
ment of a man worthy to inhabit the earth. He is born
with a shell."[40] From the muskrat, "which gnaws its third
leg off," he can learn another lesson, equally unpleasant,
about "our kindred mortality. . . . Are we not made its
brothers by fate?"[41] And then there is the *exemplum* of
fox excrement in which he finds the vertebrae and talons
of a partridge, remarking (rather ominously) that "they
are *memoires pour servir*."[42]

What *memoires*, we might ask, are provided by the
sight of "three dead suckers on the Assabet—what has
killed them?"[43] What by "the toad . . . dead on the side-
walk, flattened?"[44] What by the "shrike pecking to pieces
a small bird? I find that I had not associated such actions
with my idea of birds."[45] What by the battle of the ants,

which caused him to feel "for the rest of that day as if I had had my feelings harrowed and excited by witnessing the struggle, the ferocity and carnage, of a human battle before my door?"[46] What by walking over the tracks of a fox and rabbit struggle? Only that "we unwillingly traverse the scenery of what tragedies. Every square rod, perchance, was the scene of a life or death struggle last night."[47] Of what even in the lyrical destiny of the bee? —The bee which has been about "the Rape of the Flower! It knew where the sweet lay, and was unscrupulous in his mode of obtaining it. A certain violence tolerated by nature."[48]

Indeed, what memory or meaning other than nature's tolerance of violence can be found beneath the external loveliness of the world? Noticing a dead toad, entrails extracted, fly-encrusted, Thoreau remarks: "Such is Nature, who gave one creature a taste or yearning for another's entrails."[49] That, surely, is a *memoire pour servir*. Oversimplified and seen starkly, the scene is merely "chaos and old night." In context, however disturbing to surface serenity, it does have a meaning. We can even be "cheered" when we watch the vulture at his dinner of flesh because his "strong appetite which so disgusts and disheartens us" is yet another proof of "the inviolable health of nature." Without underestimating or glossing over this pattern of evil, in it we can "see that nature is so rife with life that myriads can be afforded to be sacrificed."[50] This is a matter for rejoicing as well as for anguishing. On the other hand, it must be admitted, this sacrifice remains as mysterious as it is inexorable. And so we must continue to question:

What becomes of all these birds that people the air and forest for our solacement? We do not see their bodies lie about. Yet there is a tragedy at the end of each one of their lives. They must perish miserably, and not one of them is translated. True, not a sparrow falleth to the ground without our Heavenly Father's knowledge, but they do fall, nevertheless.[51]

Nature is indeed terrible and terrifying. She also terrorizes man; Thoreau saw the most frightening examples of this in the ocean. "The annals of this voracious beach!" he said. "Think of the amount of suffering which a single strand has witnessed."[52] Or, heading out to sea, he found the spectacle even more frightening: "There must be something monstrous . . . in a vision of the sea bottom . . . a drowned continent all livid and frothing at the nostrils. . . ."[53] And yet, horrible as the sight and the thought might be, Thoreau reminds us of two things: that drowned men make good manure (thus does man serve nature), and that sea tragedies regularly occur which, for all man's humanism, do not produce "a visible vibration in the fabric of society."[54] Man has no excuse for his indifference. Nature's cruelties may have a purpose. For this reason Thoreau ultimately "sympathizes with the winds and waves, as if to toss and mangle these poor human bodies was the order of the day. If this was the law of Nature, why waste any time in awe or pity?"[55]

Let us study this law, he seems to say, and learn its lessons. First, it is a law unto itself, and on its own terms is just: "Only Nature has the right to grieve perpetually, for she only is innocent."[56] Second, its ways, different from man's ways, have their own ethics and aesthetics. For example, "It is remarkable that those flowers [the water lily], which are most emblematical of purity, should grow in the mud."[57] Nature creates a flower which fills "the lowlands with the odor of carrion," as if to remind man that "just so much beauty and virtue as there are in the world, and just so much ugliness and vice, you see expressed in flowers."[58] Third, her methodology is always compensatory. Thus the "withered leaves" of a skunk cabbage "are transfixed by a rising bud."[59] Thus, also, the earth should not be regarded "as a graveyard, a necropolis," but as a "granary filled with the seeds of life. Is not its fertility increased by this decay?"[60] We may call decay evil, but let us realize that it is "of venerable antiquity," that it "proves its necessity," and that "it is part of the order, not disorder, of the universe."[61]

There is a moral message to nature's evil. We should

realize that there is "an animal in us . . . reptile and sensuous"[62] even when we aspire to higher selves. We should realize that we imitate the very nature we would upbraid. For example, "It is with the graves of trees as with those of men—at first an upright stump [for a monument], in course of time a mere mound, and finally, when the corpse has decayed and shrunk, a depression in the soil."[63] This is naturalism, not fatalism. We should realize that the meaning of nature is life, not death, that its chief characteristic is "an inextinguishable vitality" most clearly seen in its patterns of renewal out of decay.[64] Even deaths in nature have purpose: "They teach us how to die. One wonders if the time will ever come when men, with their boasted faith in immortality, will ever lie down as gracefully and as ripe."[65]

Thus in giving witness to the terror in nature Thoreau is not a necrophiliac. He said that he was "not competent to write the poetry of the grave," that the fertility of decay and death is actually one of nature's economies.[66] These only are relevant to man's life. And if the only way their relevance can be discovered is through terror, then so be it: "Long enough I had heard of irrelevant things; now at length I was glad to make acquaintance with the light that dwells in rotten wood."[67] It is rotten, it may be termed evil, and it certainly seems to manifest "chaos and old night," but it is relevant, it is significant, and there is life within its death.

Sin, pain, death, and the terror in nature were Thoreau's confrontations with evil. He did not flinch. Real is real. However, he did manage to translate the real into rather more ideal terms.

Hating superficiality, he embraced what others reject: "The moaning of the storm gives me pleasure. Methinks it is because it puts to rout the trivialness of our fair-weather life and gives it at least a tragic interest."[68] He stood up for "a hard and base life" because "I find my last consolation in its untrivialness."[69] He went out to the mortality of nature, reading his own there: "Dead trees, sere leaves, dried grass and herbs—are not these a good part of our life?"[70] In even the "dreariness" of life he could detect "a pure and unqualified strain of eternal melody, . . . a dirge to one household, . . . a morning song of rejoicing to another."[71] Finally, as he even contemplated that death (of his brother John) which came close to shattering him, he could conclude: "What right have I to grieve who have not ceased to wonder?"[72]

Wonder, not despite but because of all the manifestations of "chaos and old night," clears away the artificialities of life, helps man to take life seriously at last, turns him into a poet and philosopher in whom "there really never is any moonshine, . . . no hard times or failures, for they deal with permanent values."[73] Dark wonder, then, confirms the possibilities of life. So when Thoreau says, "Greater is the depth of sadness / Than is any height of gladness,"[74] he does not mean that evil overwhelms the good in life. He does mean that the wonder at evil ultimately discloses both the good and the glad because it discloses the real life of life. He pays a price for the disclosure. What he purchases—an appreciation of life —is priceless, however, in any fundamental sense. It is this sense, with its wonder, not its simple terror, that he passes on to us.

Disciplined to value life, we may then go on to discover the ground of our being and the source of our joy—nature. Having learned how to read life, to realize the self, and to develop purpose, we are not allowed to go on to more permanent and positive aspects of Thoreau's thought until he has taught us how we set back life and how life sets us back. However, once taught, that is, both initiated and tried, we are allowed to move on.

Our direction is upward. Nature is the platform from which we begin the ascent.

PART III:

CONVICTION

Chapter 7

GROUND OF NATURE:
"IN HEYWOOD'S MEADOW"

Myrica, not quite. Lousewort pollen, how long?[1]

But unconsidered expressions of our delight which any natural object draws from us are something complete and final in themselves, since all nature is to be regarded as it concerns man.[2]

Enjoying an original relationship with nature, Thoreau did not much care how his contemporaries defined his professional interest. Was this scientific? To a certain extent. Largely self-taught, he did manage to amass a considerable body of accurate knowledge about botany, ornithology, forest ecology, and animal lore. Pragmatic? At least to the degree of learning how to live off the land both in and out of season. Poetic? Indeed, what he saw and heard in his world frequently appealed to him in terms of feeling and imagination, of cadence and trope, and was often expressed by him in those terms. Philosophic? Partly, although he did not set out deliberately to elicit a thought system from nature or to foist one upon it. Moralistic? Again, in part, so long as it is understood that, in his judgment, the universe wanted aestheticians more than it wanted ethicians, and simple, joyful observers more than aestheticians.

What his real interest was, perhaps, has no name. That nature was demonstrably the most important force in his life is all that really matters—to him or to us. How he treated nature, or (in a manner of speaking) how nature treated him, attests to this force and explains it. Required of us, then, is an account of this treatment: that is, an observation of him observing.

Many of his finest prose passages may supply this requirement: the seascapes of *Cape Cod;* the mountain views of *Maine Woods;* the "Brute Neighbors" or "Sounds" chapters of *Walden;* more technically, either his quite original "The Succession of Forest Trees," or his detailed, informed review of *The Natural History of Massachusetts;* less formally, the thousands of journal entries recording, transcendentally as well as factually, the wonders which his Concord wayside ramblings turned up for him. However, we can do no better than to study his work in "Autumnal Tints,"[3] for here at once he is most simple and profound, most scientific and merely hedonistic, most concerned to make very specific and significant the kinship of man and nature.

He opens the essay with a reference to what might be called America's secret and delightfully unexpected wealth, one which is not usually figured into or numbered among her natural resources, much less in her treasury reports. That wealth is the brilliance and variety of the fall foliage. And yet, he pines, "October has hardly tinged our poetry." If we notice the fruits of this month at all, it is likely to be in the measurement of the apple harvest or in our depression that summer has too soon ended. As for our trade, we should be aware that nature ripens for us a show of fruits we never dreamed of—and do not see—because we think only of those we can eat. As for our spirits, confusing "changed leaves" with "withered ones" is like mistaking the ripe for the rotten, whereas we might better understand the look of a turned or turning tree as a sign of "late and perfect maturity." (Scientists, of course, have another and less poetic explanation for this phenomenon—but "I'm more interested in the rosy cheek than I am to know what particular diet the maiden fed on.")

Thoreau's introduction is, however, more than an introduction. In a sense, it is all he wishes to say, not so much about this or any other aspect of nature, as about the way in which man ought to take nature. Assured that we can tell the difference between a fact and a poem, between a gift and a right, he then carries us forth—

chronologically, from late August to early December; botanically, from the grasses to the tops of the tallest trees; and, artistically, from the greenish purples to the reddish yellows.

His guided tour is factual enough, with its dates, classifications, Latin terminology, and meticulous, almost scrupulous, attention to detail. But the best of the tour may be found in what to any other guide would be the asides. To Thoreau, never a typical guide to anything, the slant line is always the straightest.

Leaves suggest to him, and he suggests to us, that nature's way is to plant the uncommon among the common (colorful grasses, for example, amid the end-of-summer browns and dead greens); to distinguish always between use and beauty; to propose a vintage "not confined to the vine." The fields and low forests are a refuge "before August is over, from college commencements and society that isolates," as well as a constant source of mythology and poetry. In addition, should one be as concerned for implications as for data, he can learn religious lessons in the spectacle as good as any in the Bible. For example, similar to the "first shall be last, last first" parable is the case of the red maple. Throughout the year these trees were shy and retiring, performing their daily duties unnoticed, working steadily and unglamorously, not seeming to prosper, all the while husbanding their sap. Then, suddenly, they come into their own as "burning bushes"—deserving well of mapledom and at last capable of leading the traveler from the dusty road to "brave solitudes."

Nature, Thoreau continues, is good for man. It is his joy, the lavish gift of an uninhibited deity. How does it get away with the exuberance and audacity of its lavishness?

One wonders that the tithing man and fathers of the town are not out to see what the trees mean by their high colors and exuberance of spirits, fearing that some mischief is brewing. I do not see what the

Puritans did at this season, when the maples blaze
out in scarlet. They certainly could not have wor-
shiped in groves then. Perhaps that is why they
built meeting-houses and fenced them round with
horse-sheds.[4]

In the same ironic tone, having beheld with delight a
flourishing sugar maple in the yard of a country parish,
he asks: "What meant the fathers by establishing this
perfectly living institution before the church?" The answer is that, to all who will hear their word, the trees
are "cheap preachers." But if nature is good for man, not
all men are good for nature. They fail to respond with joy
to nature's joy. Take the market-man, for instance,

> . . . driving into the village, and disappearing under
> the canopy of elm-tops, with his crop. I am tempted
> to go thither as to a husking of thoughts, now dry
> and ripe, and ready to be separated from their
> integuments; but, alas! I foresee that it will be
> chiefly husks and little thoughts, blasted pig-corn,
> fit only for cob-meal—for, as you sow, so shall you
> reap.[5]

Thoreau concludes his (by now) more moral than natural observations with two sentiments, one autobiograph-
ical and the other philosophical–theological, which have a
bearing on the proper approach to nature and leave-taking
from nature. Both of these effectively prepare his audience for an understanding of everything he could possibly
tell them about nature. Out of his own experience, first,
he tells us this:

> In my botanical rambles I find that first, the idea,
> or image of a plant occupies my thoughts, . . . and
> for some weeks or months I go thinking of it and at
> length I surely see it. This is the history of my find-
> ing a score or more rare plants. . . . A man sees only
> what concerns him.[6]

The point is simply this: although nature is fantastically bountiful, her gifts must be sought for, prepared for, asked for. Man must train, so to speak, to receive her blessings. Second, man must learn how to take leave of nature's majesty, how to say thank you for each benediction. This will be most efficaciously accomplished if he will realize (and live accordingly) that everything in nature has some beauty and some use, that in her economy there is no waste, that her greatest majesty is manifested in her humblest subjects, and that all her pronouncements are ultimately moral. And so Thoreau reminds man that "these bright leaves which I have mentioned are not the exception, but the rule; for I believe that all leaves, even grasses and mosses, acquire higher colors just before they fall." The point is: take notice of what is least noticeable.

For Thoreau the notice began in his immediate surroundings. Although, he said, "there is a still life in America that is little observed or dreamed of,"[7] having done some traveling (and imagining the natural riches of the territories he had not visited), he preferred the near to the far, New England to the great regions of the South and West. As he put the matter, "Dear to me to lie in this sand; fit to preserve the bones of a race for thousands of years to come. And this is my home, my native soil; and I am a New Englander. . . . Here have I my habitat. I am of thee."[8] Others might disparage this place—because it is near and therefore not exotic—but for him it will suffice. It sustains him, despite the supposed vulgarity of its nutriment: "Do not think that the fruits of New England are mean and insignificant. . . . They educate us, and fit us to live in New England."[9] And when he exclaimed, in a marvelously joyful, transcendental ode to snow crystals, "What a world we live in!" because, nothing "cheap or coarse" in it, it seemed "full of genius, full of the divinity,"[10] he was not referring to one of nature's monumental achievements in some romantic land but to what she provided, day after day, on a small scale as near as one's own vantage point, wherever that happened to be. In fact, it was very likely to be in one's own neighborhood, for Thoreau as close as "Heywood's meadow" where "I had no idea that there was so much going on."[11]

The natural activity there is what counts, not that it is near, certainly not that it fails to announce itself loudly. But because it is near, "I am compelled to look at near objects. All things have a soothing effect. . . . My power of observation and contemplation is much increased. My attention does not wander. . . . What now of Europe and Asia?"[12] Because it is near, he can immerse himself in ready details, to a certain extent thereby losing "sight of the ultimate uses" but gaining immensely because "the immediate ones are so great."[13] Because it is near, he could devote himself, in the manner of a Wordsworth rather than of a Coleridge, to what in nature matters most because it happens more often. Thus he would "omit the unusual—the hurricanes and earthquakes—and describe the common. This has the greatest charm and is the true theme of poetry."[14]

To be a scientific naturalist, then, a philosopher–poet, or simply an interested, interesting human being, he needed no more activity than that which went on "in Heywood's meadow." What did go on there, at least as he discovered it, was nothing more than nature's normal routine, nothing less than an invitation, as warm as it was constant, to wonder and to enjoy:

> Consider what actual phenomena await us. To say nothing of life, which may be rare and difficult to detect, and death, which is startling enough, we cannot begin to conceive of anything so surprisingly thrilling but that something more surprising may be actually presented to us.[15]

All this is there "in Heywood's meadow." The trick is how to get at it. We learn this trick by first realizing how not to get it. Heywood, for example, might not get it because he is possessive of externals only, whereas the trespassing Irishman (a bit of a poacher) might get it because he is more fundamentally practical, less possessive. Of the first, Thoreau asks this question: "Does he chiefly own the land who coldly uses it and gets corn and potatoes out of it, or he who loves it and gets inspiration from it?"[16] In defense of the latter, he simply declares: "The highest law gives a thing to him who can use it."[17]

What is the "use" of a phenomenon? Whatever it is, Thoreau warned in the best Romantic tradition, a scientist will not discover it. And because he won't, the real riches of Heywood's meadow will be lost to him and on him. Thoreau is quite insistent on this point. Scientists, he said, are prone to facts. But "a fact stated barely is dry. It must be the vehicle of some humanity in order to interest us. Ultimately, the moral is all in all. . . . It must be warm, moist, incarnated,—have been breathed on at least. A man has not seen a thing who has not felt it."[18] A scientist sins and falters in the name and interest of objectivity. It is his mistake to "coolly give [his] chief attention to the phenomenon which excites [him] as something independent of [him] and not as it is related to [him]. The important fact is its effect on me. It is the subject of a vision, the truth alone, that concerns me."[19] And the scientist is dangerously, blindingly blunt, much too forthright for his own good: "Man cannot afford to be a naturalist, to look at nature directly, but only with the side of his eye. He must look through and beyond her. To look at her is fatal as to look at the head of Medusa. It turns the man of science into stone."[20]

It is Thoreau's considered advice, then, to approach nature naturally. Go forth not "consciously as an observer, but in the fullness of life" if you expect nature "to make her report to you."[21] What is required is "a true sauntering of the eye," not a professional scrutiny.[22] Therefore, "if you would obtain insight, avoid anatomy."[23] You should move with the grace and instinct of a poet. He alone knows "the truest use of the pine who does not fondle it with an axe, nor tickle it with a saw, nor stroke it with a plane, who knows whether its heart is false without cutting into it."[24] You should be a lover, plain and simple: "In Boston yesterday an ornithologist said significantly, 'If you held the bird in your hand—'; but I would rather hold it in my affections."[25]

Now it is not quite true to assert, or to present Thoreau as asserting, a total rejection of the scientific method. While he said, "I fear that the dream of the toads will not sound so musical now that I know whence it proceeds," he avowed in the same context, "I will not fear to know."[26] The important thing is merely to put scientific knowledge into perspective. If, for example, "our books in science, as they improve in accuracy, are in danger of losing the freshness and vigor and readiness to appreciate the real laws of Nature,"[27] then the scientific method has obviously been misused. If we put "an eagle in captivity, screaming in a courtyard," in order to study him where he does not belong, then we have abused nature. What is more, Thoreau asserted, "I am not the wiser respecting eagles for having seen one there. I do not wish to know the length of its entrails."[28] Quite simply, if in learning the "numbers and names of each order" of creation we lose rather than gain respect for the "variety and fertility in nature,"[29] we have failed both to understand and to appreciate the splendid possibilities of our relation to nature—"in Heywood's meadow."

Two final passages of admonition will summarize Thoreau's judgment of how not to seek the treasures of that meadow:

> In science, I should say, all description is postponed till we know the whole, but then science itself will be cast aside. But unconsidered expressions of our delight which any natural object draws from us are something complete and final in themselves, since all nature is to be regarded as it concerns man; and who knows how near to absolute truth such unconscious affirmation may come?[30]

The message here is to be simple, to enjoy, and to conduct yourself humanly in the meadow. Otherwise you will know it but will neither understand nor appreciate it. Moreover, as you approach the phenomena of that place, bear in mind that

... the mystery of the life of plants is kindred with that of our own lives, and the physiologist must not presume to explain their growth according to mechanical laws. ... We must not expect to probe with our fingers the sanctuary of any life.[31]

In a word, treat nature as you would be treated: reverently, humanly, gently.

Conversely, if impersonal objectivity does not make for an appropriate vestibule to the temple of Heywood's meadow (where the sacred mysteries are enacted daily), a warmly subjective, distinctly human approach would be the ritually correct entrance. Three reasons—a positive, a negative, and a neutral one—will explain why. First, whatever is decent and attractive in a man will correspond to and find correspondences in similar qualities in nature. Thoreau comes close to the pathetic fallacy, as did many another Romantic, in this point of view; but it is expressed by him, just as it is to be taken by us, as a literal, not just a figurative, truth. As he put it: "Nature must be viewed humanly to be viewed at all; that is, her scenes must be associated with human affections, such as are associated with one's native place. ... She is most significant to a lover."[32] Second, whatever is morally repellent in man will find its counterpart in nature's (occasional) ugliness. Thoreau suggests, it is true, somewhat in the fashion of Balzac's "Passion in the Desert," that man corrupts nature rather than nature corrupting man. The point is, however, that there is a double corruption. Thus, he says, "Not only foul and poisonous weeds grow in our tracks, but our vileness and luxuriance make simple and wholesome plants rank and weed-like."[33] Third, whether or not we may see both our virtue and our vice reflected in nature's mirror, the fact would still be that even our most private and unique faculties—our sensibilities and sensitivities—derive from objects in the natural world about us. "Talk about learning our letters and being literate!" Thoreau reminds us. "Why, the roots of letters are things. Natural objects and phenomena are the original symbols or types which express our thoughts and feelings."[34] This being the case, it follows that to approach nature humanly is to approach it humbly, giving credit where credit is due, returning thanks for favors received, and rediscovering the very origins, for good or bad, of our human life in the natural life. In short, to be natural is to be human; to be human is to be natural.

Explanations apart, however, Thoreau is quite explicit on the necessity of a human attendance on nature. Again and again he stresses this point. For example, thinking about the recurring bounties of the course of months, he remarks, "The seasons were not made in vain. . . . It is for man the seasons and all their fruits exist."[35] Or, contemplating an exercise in strictly natural history, he realizes the human dimensions of his subject: "I did not see why I might not make a book on Cape Cod, as well as my neighbor on 'Human Culture.' It is but another name for the same thing."[36] Or, clearly attuned to nature's silent strains, he urges the necessity of a human response to the melody, as when he asks, "Who hears the fishes when they cry? It will not be forgotten by some memory that we were contemporaries."[37] Briefly, then, although nature can manage without man, he cannot manage without her. This is to say that, unless he goes to her personally, expecting to meet there a person rather than a thing, Heywood's meadow will not respond to him, will not even exist for him. For "what is nature unless there is an eventful human life passing within her?"[38]

So, then, we go to nature humanly. But the humanity we bring there must be the very best self possible. Echoing, perhaps, the "visible saint" notion of the Puritans (the notion that a church does not save; rather it exists for the saved), Thoreau will have it that only the pure can receive what nature has to give. Her question is: "Are you virtuous? Then you can behold me."[39] The reason for this is that "Nature does not cast pearls before swine. There is just as much beauty [or virtue] visible to us in the landscape as we are prepared to appreciate,— and not a grain more."[40] We may seek in nature the "preservation of moral and intellectual health,"[41] but unless we possess this health in some degree we will be refused admission to what he calls the *"sanctum sanctorum, . . . the penetralia* of the temple . . . [which] are the broad noon of our existence."[42] If nature leaves us bare and dry, it is because we are that way. Thoreau had such days when "nature looked uncommonly bare and dry," but he ascribed the condition of nature to his own condition, reading into the former "our own physical and corresponding moral revolutions." Therefore, he concluded that the ugliness he saw came from his soul, not his sight—for "the perception of beauty is a moral test."[43] He further concluded that "a man receives only what he is ready to receive . . . as animals conceive at certain seasons their kind only."[44] Thus if "objects are concealed from our view," the trouble is that "there is no intention of the mind and eye toward them."[45] And if, finally, we do not find in nature our expectation of a better life, the fault is ours in that the majestic never seems majestic to the mean. Thus, "Nature is beautiful only as a place where a life is to be lived. It is not beautiful to him who has not resolved on a beautiful life."[46]

In a manner of speaking, then, both beauty and virtue are in the mind of the beholder of nature. More precisely, beauty and virtue are as beauty and virtue do. It would follow that the majority of men, blind to beauty and hardened to virtue, cannot expect to see nature clearly and to see it whole. They never realize its "eternal health and beauty" because their petty grievances afford them "only transient and partial glimpses."[47] They behave "like oxen in a flower-garden," failing to appreciate that "the true fruit of Nature can only be plucked with a delicate hand."[48] And they

. . . nowhere, east or west, live yet a natural life, round which the vine clings and which the elm willingly shadows. Man would desecrate it by his touch, and so the beauty of the world remains veiled to him. He needs not only to be spiritualized, but naturalized, on the soil of the earth.[49]

On the other hand, properly disposed and fitly motivated, man may be said to enjoy perfect health, the only kind tolerated by nature. Once he has offered this health to nature, his remaining task is to ensure it and maintain it. This he may do, this he is now permitted to do, by establishing a "very near personal" relationship with nature:

> He must be conscious of a friendliness in her; when human friends fail or die, she must stand in the gap to him. . . . Unless Nature sympathizes with and speaks to us, the most fertile and blooming regions are barren and dreary.[50]

With nature now sympathetic to his needs, man can proceed to a full satisfaction of them "in Heywood's meadow." These chiefly are psychological: the need for joy and wonder, the need for consolation and hope, and the need for, let us call it, life-confidence.

Joy is as small a thing as a fine day: "How perfectly new and fresh the world is seen to be, when we behold a myriad sparkles of brilliant white sunlight on a rippled stream! So remote from dust and decay, more bright than the flash of an eye."[51] It is the sound of a thrush: "Whenever a man hears it, he is young, and Nature is in her spring."[52] It is the song of the blackbird, changing "all hours to an eternal morning," banishing "all trivialness," and reinstating man in his dominion.[53] It is a cricket's chirrup, the "superior strains" of which set him "to thinking, philosophizing, moralizing," and the message of which, directed at mere summer "time-servers," annihilates time and space."[54] It is the "utterly uncivilized" hoot of an owl who is "plainly not nervous about his solitary life, nor afraid to hear the echo of his voice there,"[55] whose "idiotic and maniacal" cry suggests "a vast undeveloped nature which men have not recognized."[56] Above all, it is the extraordinary grandeur of one of the last of nature's darlings:

> I know of no object more unsightly to careless glance than an empty thistle-head, yet, if you examine it

closely, it may remind you of the silk-lined cradle in which a prince was rocked. Thus that which seemed a mere brown and worn-out relic of summer, sinking into the earth by the roadside, turns out to be a precious casket.[57]

Unfortunately, man is not always open to wonder and joy. Given the fact that there is "absolute barrenness" to be found in none of nature's dominions but fecundity and vitality everywhere, he has absolutely "no excuse for peevishness."[58] Peevish he is, nevertheless. Sometimes this may be because with him "all is uncertainty. He does not look forward to another spring." Then does nature put forth her peculiar form of consolation—in, for example, the root of the aster, dirt-covered and buried deep, where "you will find the new shoots."[59] Sometimes it may be because he is troubled by thoughts of death. Now let nature prove to him that "the earth is not a mere fragment of dead history . . . but living poetry, like the leaves of a tree which precede flowers and fruit." Let her then refresh and recreate him out of her "inexhaustible vigor." For "we need to witness our own limits transgressed, and some life pasturing freely where we never wander."[60] And if he perchance has doubts about immortality, let him predicate of himself "the eternity which I detect in Nature." Let him read her "steady persistency and recovery" into his own future.[61] In short, whenever man is depressed or troubled, let him see nature as the physician to his soul. Let him do as Thoreau did: "This stillness, solitude, wildness of nature is a kind of thoroughwort, or boneset, to my intellect. This is what I go out to seek."[62]

Finally, the confidence which nature inspires goes beyond simple joy, exceeds mere consolation. It is something elemental and fundamental. It is absolute. Whether he knows it or not, ephemeral man has a tremendous psychological need for such qualities. In nature's supreme confidence he can discover his own certainty and stability, or at least a consistent, reliable source of them. Two typical passages will indicate both Thoreau's serenity and the security which he feels nature holds out to all men. "While I bask in the sun on the shores of Walden Pond," he tells us, "by this heat and this rustle I am absolved from all obligation to the past. The council of nations may reconsider their votes; the grating of a pebble annuls them."[63] This is not a pantheistic oneness with nature, nor is it a transcendental attempt to absorb the divinity posited by nature. It is, rather, a perfect contentment with nature and a reliance on it. Similarly, if somewhat less profoundly, his statement on the stolidness of earth sets the weakness of man in sharp perspective:

> What events have transpired on the lit and airy surface three inches above them! Summer knocked down; Kansas living in an age of suspense. Think what is a summer to them! How many worthy men have died . . . since I saw the mother turtle bury her eggs here! . . . Be not in haste; mind your private affairs. A whole summer is not too good nor too much to hatch a turtle in. . . . French empires rise or fall, but the turtle is developed only so fast.[64]

The turtle, of course (this is his point), develops according to a law, "steadily advancing toward maturity, all nature abetting." It convinces Thoreau of what he calls "an irresistible necessity for mud turtles." More important, it suggests "with what tenacity Nature sticks to her idea."[65] Law, necessity, idea: it is these terms which recur in Thoreau's final, most profound identification of nature as the ground of all being, and in his doctrine of nature as the ground of man's particular being. It is this ground which supplies, one might say, the highest (or most basic) use of nature—a use which obtains whether or not man accepts it but which gives total meaning to his life if he does.

Every object in nature reveals the ground and suggests the use. "The lapse of the current" in the stream, for example, is "an emblem of all progress, following the same law with the system, with time, and all that is made."[66] A single rill of melted snow points to "the laws by which the world was made, and according to which the systems revolve."[67] A "poor worm's instinct" is not merely that, but "the mind of the universe. All the wit in the world was brought to bear on each case to secure its end."[68] Even the "simplest and most lumpish fungus," with neither use nor appeal to most men, "is the expression of an idea." That idea, *in fine,* is "growth according to law."[69]

What does the law teach man? Basic facts and universal correspondences. That the earth one walks, hardly an inert mass, "has a spirit" and is "fluid to the influence of its spirit, and to whatever particle of that spirit resides in man."[70] That in nature "nothing is wasted" because everything that decays (and all must decay) is simply rendered "the better fitted to serve in some other department."[71] That nature always represents what man rarely achieves—"perfect confidence and success." Why, even her winter's snow is "not an evil to be corrected." Rather, "it is as it was designed and made to be, for the artist has had leisure to add beauty to use."[72]

Nature, in her laws, not despite them, is then "mythical and mystical always, and works with the license and extravagance of genius."[73] For her laws point always to life and only to life: the life in Heywood's meadow, the life of men, and the suggestion of life (as principle or spirit, as idea or ideal) which underlies these lives. We are encouraged to know and to love her laws because by them we both live and find meaning in life. Fortunately for us, it is not difficult to be lawful:

> Surely the fates are forever kind, though Nature's laws are more immutable than any despot's, yet to man's daily life they rarely seem rigid. . . . He is not harshly reminded of the things he may not do.[74]

How may we acknowledge our devotion to these laws, hence our dedication to life? On a natural plane, not unduly facetiously, Thoreau suggests that we declare a holiday in honor of squirrels. We treat them as vermin and hunt them down, but they admirably perform a "legal"

function as "'planters of forests." Therefore, "Would it
not be far more civilized and humane, not to say godlike,
to recognize once in a year by some significant symbolical ceremony the part which the squirrel plays, the
great service it performs, in the economy of the universe?"[75] Or, on a very human level, we might tell some
little boy, chagrined because he has dropped the berry
basket, what Thoreau told Edward Emerson—in kindness
and in truth:

> Nature had provided that little boys should now and
> then stumble and sow the berries. We shall have a
> grand lot of bushes and berries in this spot, and we
> shall owe them to you.[76]

Since nature works through little boys and squirrels,
such holidays and such consolations would be eminent
proof that we had accepted and rejoiced in her laws,
that we were in fact affirming the life (in growth) to
which these laws direct us, that we had learned the lesson
of Heywood's meadow. At the very least, these simple
actions would be our way of uniting the ground of our
being and the ground of existence itself.

In that union and on that ground we may come into
our own. Schooled by the master teacher, which is the
universe, we may now begin to discover and to practice
those virtues essential to our (now) exalted lives. These
are the virtues of freedom and simplicity—nature's own
virtues.

Chapter 8

FREEDOM AND SIMPLICITY:
"AN INVISIBLE NETWORK OF
SPECULATIONS"

If you can drive a nail and have any nails to drive,
drive them.[1]

Do we call this the land of the free? What is it to be
born free . . . and not to live? We quarter troops
upon ourselves.[2]

The nature which Thoreau put forth for our consideration
was, of course, an objective reality in the sense that it
existed and worked on and for mankind pretty much as
he described it and its operation. On the other hand, as
we can readily see, it was interpreted subjectively with
the intention that it be understood in the same manner.
Thoreau shared, even if he did not precisely borrow, the
attitudes toward nature of Lucretius and Humboldt, of
Camoens and the nineteenth-century British poets, of the
Oriental mystics and the Concord seers. Ultimately and
essentially, however, his point of view was distinctly
and distinctively his own.

Occasionally, it might appear, he would search out
and present a natural philosophy which in most respects
he could accept and recommend—if only to take such an
opportunity to declare his modicum of reservation or dis-
agreement. The acceptance would be gratefully acknowledged, the recommendation freely given. The modicum
of dubiety, however, is of greater significance because it
is this which announces the uniqueness of his own program.

A good example of this particular methodology of
agreeing to disagree may be found in a lengthy, judicious

review he wrote of the second British edition (London, 1842) of a popular German work: J. A. Etzler's pretentiously, portentously titled book, *The Paradise Within the Reach of All Men, Without Labor, by Powers of Nature and Machinery—An Address to All Intelligent Men.* The title of Thoreau's piece, more simply and trenchantly, was "Paradise [to be] Regained."[3]

Noting at the outset that Etzler's material was doctrinally derivative (chiefly from Fourier), he admitted that "it did expand us a little." After all, he said, there is such a thing as—and a need for—"transcendentalism in mechanics as well as in ethics." Indeed, he also said in apparent approval, "While one reformer scours the heavens, the other sweeps the earth." So far, so good.

Presumably paraphrasing Etzler, still with approval, Thoreau goes on to indicate the scope and use of the book before him. Men have inherited a "fair homestead," it is true, but they have done little to improve it, so minimally have they "cleared and hedged and ditched." Much remains to be done: "to wash water, and warm fire, and cool ice, and underprop the earth"; "to teach birds to fly and fishes to swim"; and in general to naturalize nature. At the very least, even if we fail in such enterprises, "it is time we looked into these things." What is more, insofar as Etzler (obviously sympathetic to nature and urgently proposing a closer man–nature relationship) has reminded us of "the innumerable and immeasurable powers" which are ready to work for us, he has done us a service. Thoreau would be the first to agree with and the last to deny the untapped uses of the wind, the tide, the waves, and the sunshine. With the help of these things, he says, our "question is not how we shall execute but what. Let us not use in a niggardly manner what is thus generously offered."

In fact, Thoreau remains on Etzler's side until he gets to the matter of purpose. One would have thought this to be "simplify, simplify," Thoreau's own formula for the good life. What, then, can be wrong with a thesis, particularly one based on nature's proposals, which says that "all labor shall be reduced to a 'short turn of some crank' "? What is wrong, says Thoreau, is the crank—because a crank requires a crank-turner. Etzler goes far, but not far enough for Thoreau. He believes in simplicity, but not in complete simplicity. He would try to liberate man, but he would not give him full freedom. He puts forth a reliance on nature, but not an absolute reliance. For just one crank suggests the mechanical and the artificial, the needlessly complex, demanding master of an otherwise free man.

Lest he seem unduly cranky about the efforts of a fellow naturalist to improve life, Thoreau digs more deeply into the flaws of Etzler's system. For one thing, all of his propositions will require men, money, and time. "Alas," says Thoreau, "this is the crying sin of the age, this want of faith in the prevalence of *a* man. Nothing can be effected but by *one* man. He who wants help wants everything." As for money, faith (not funds) is sufficient to underwrite any worthwhile project. Time? No time at all, for "the Divine is about to be."

Etzler dreams grandly but not grandly enough, and "his castles in the air fall to the ground because they are not built lofty enough." One proof of his lack of stature, for all the expansiveness of his theme, is that he "aims to secure the greatest degree of gross comfort and pleasure merely." He is no idealist. Another proof is that he obviously is not committed to the liberating influences of instinct and spirit; rather, he turns out to be an organizer, a manipulator, a mechanic. But, surely, says Thoreau, "there is a speedier way than 'the mechanical system' to fill up marshes, to drown the roar of the waves, . . . and that is by the power of rectitude and true behavior." Finally, to Thoreau's way of thinking at any rate, Etzler ultimately proves himself false to both nature and the supranatural when he asserts that the principles of science should be applied to man's morals. Reality demands the reverse of this application, for "there are truths in physics because they are true in ethics."

In a word, Etzler was not a virtuous man. He was a mechanic. He had the world neatly figured out. But to Thoreau, a self-styled "hypaethral" naturalist (that is, under the ether), Etzler smelled of the library, whence comes no true morality.[4] He reduced life to a diagram on a drawing board, thus missing those "flitting perspectives and demi-experiences" which are "outside to time" and yet "perennial in the wind and rain which never die."[5] He had a plan for life, but he did not live.

To live, that is to live virtuously and therefore abundantly, one needed not systems but two virtues only: freedom and simplicity. Both, in Thoreau's scheme, have secondary meanings and double connotations. By freedom he meant, in addition to the usual readings of the term, the kind of exemption (from duty, from systems, from social obligations) which solitude alone afforded. In solitude man was free to be himself. A loftier conception of freedom, or use thereof, Thoreau could not imagine. By simplicity, he meant to signify what might ordinarily be called sincerity—the quality of being true to oneself rather than to codes, customs, or mechanical procedures. Sincerity complements freedom in the way that insincerity always complements—and is a requirement of—social complexity and restraint.

Furthermore, freedom suggests something positive as well as something negative. The free man is for something as well as against something. He must take a stand against servitude and servility in all their many forms (social, intellectual, and personal, as well as political and economic); he should also take a stand on uninhibition, uniqueness, the wildness of genius and the genius of wildness. Biblically, "the truth shall make him free"—that is, the truth which solitude discloses to him. Similarly, simplicity argues against complexity, but it must also argue for the absolute value of clean, clear purpose in life. Biblically, again, Thoreau seems to be saying that, since we come into this world and go out of it naked, so must we spend the time between in devotion to essentials only, the essentials of one's private business on earth.

Etzler, in the name of natural liberation, would tie a man to a system. And, under the auspices of a simplified way of life, he would further complicate man's already intricate existence. But Thoreau proposes not only a refutation of Etzler but also the positive position of a real life of virtue. Freedom and simplicity are that life.

Freedom

THe fact must be faced that Thoreau's theory and practice of freedom have a selfish, arrogant look. If there was an explanation for this, perhaps in an ideal which realists could not penetrate, certainly his contemporaries —those who knew him best and were inclined to sympathize with him the most—failed to find one. Isaac Hecker, for example, himself a ruggedly individualistic, freedom-jealous personalist, once said of him:

Under his seeming truthfulness and frankness he conceals an immense amount of pride, pretention, and infidelity. This tendency to solitude and asceticism means something, and there is a certain degree of truthfulness and even bravery in his attempts to find out what this something is; but his results are increased pride, pretention, and infidelity, instead of humility, simplicity, and piety.[6]

The point seems to be that Thoreau's sense of personal freedom, however well motivated originally, degenerates into an excuse for self-indulgence at the expense of both human relations and the sanctity of freedom itself. A certain event in his life supports the Hecker judgment as well as adding to it a possible diagnosis of paranoia, which in this case would mean that Thoreau's stand on freedom led him not only into isolation from the human community but also into a defiance of that community under the sick delusion of his grandeur, its unworthiness. The event was his accidentally setting fire to a tract of forest. This was his reaction:

I had felt like a guilty person, nothing but shame and regret. But now I settled the matter with myself shortly. I said to myself: "Who are these men who are said to be the owners of these woods, and how am

I related to them?" I have set fire to the forest, but I have done no wrong therein. I settled it with myself and stood to watch the approaching flames. It was a glorious spectacle, and I was the only one there to enjoy it.[7]

Hecker's words are hard and harsh. Thoreau's defense (really an offense) is far from defensible. Either his liberty had become a mere license, or else he had discovered a source of freedom, perhaps the essence of freedom, which lifts him above condemnation and by which lesser notions of freedom stand condemned as debased.

In truth he believed that he had found a pre-lapsarian state or condition, a font of paradisiacal virtue (like the virtue of freedom) which made him dissatisfied with the ordinary human life. Out of this nostalgia for paradise, so to speak, he proposed an absolute freedom, one outside and not beholden to relative (and therefore interconnected, complex) freedoms. As he put it: "We may believe it, but never do we live a quiet, free life, such as Adam's, but are enveloped in an invisible network of speculations. Our progress is from one such speculation to another, and only at rare intervals do we perceive that it is no progress. Could we for a moment drop this byplay, and simply wonder, without reference or inference?"[8] In other words, Adam was completely, absolutely free because he lived a life of pure thought, whereas other men are enmeshed in networks which oppose thought or which result in impure thought. Other men are trapped by surface complexities, whereas he would tap the freedom of the deep. Another Adam, Thoreau then proposed not only a way out of blatant slavery but a way out of subtle, invisible servitudes as well:

We always study antiques with silence and reflection. Even time has a depth, and below its surface the waves do not lapse and roar. I wonder men can be so frivolous almost as to attend to the gross form of Negro slavery, there are so many keen and subtle

masters who subject us both. Self-emancipation in
the West Indies of a man's thinking and imagining
provinces, which should be more than his island
territory—one emancipated heart and intellect. It
would knock off the fetters from a million slaves.⁹

The fact is, however, that even the new Adams, in
order to preserve their emancipated hearts and intellects,
must be prepared to deal with certain other kinds of freedom (or violations thereof)—even if by so doing they
must necessarily increase the "network of speculations."
The reason is that this is not paradise—or not yet paradise. We may identify these freedoms as political, social,
commercial, and psychological. The first is the most obvious, least important; the last is the least obvious, most
important.

To Thoreau political freedom was something transcendental. At least it transcends the law. In fact, he said,
"the law will never make men free; it is men who have
got to make the law free."¹⁰ Such a man was John Brown
—"a man of rare common sense and directness of speech
as of action; a Transcendentalist above all, a man of ideals
and principles—that was what distinguished him."¹¹ Now
other men had died for freedom, other men had been
hanged for liberating slaves. Why did Brown have such a
tremendous impact on politics, the others not? The difference, says Thoreau, is that "we were not so sure of
their devotion to principle. We made [in the case of John
Brown] a subtle distinction, forgot human laws, and did
homage to an idea. The North, I mean the living North,
was suddenly all transcendental."¹² Those in his day
could not or would not be transcendental because they
were prisoners of that "network of speculations" called
the establishment (the establishment as state or the esta-
lishment as social code). But for a Thoreau, as for a
Brown, duty to a principle was more demanding than
duty to an establishment. "Rather than thus consent to
establish hell upon earth,—to be a party to this establishment,—I would touch a match to blow up earth and
hell together."¹³ And what was this principle? Not merely

to abolish slavery but, much more important, "to do right."[14] Of such principles is political liberty made and maintained.

Thoreau's own experiences with the establishment, as recorded in "Civil Disobedience," "Slavery in Massachusetts," and "A Plea for John Brown," ostensibly were translated into discussions of personal freedom and Negro slavery. Essentially, however, these were ethical rather than political studies. Becoming increasingly strident, they first counseled the refusal to pay taxes, then endorsed violations of the fugitive slave laws, and finally militantly advocated what looks very much like treason. In each case, however, the issue was "to do right," not to forward this or that political position. Politics were strictly secondary. Moreover, the nature of the right in each instance was clearly that of the righteous freedom of the individual, of individualism itself, not the political reformation of society. The real right of freedom is only glancingly attacked by the state, frontally assaulted by the individual's failure to uphold his own individualism: "Do we call this the land of the free? What is it to be born free and equal, and not to live? We quarter troops upon ourselves."[15] As for slavery, Thoreau reminds us, "It is not the peculiar institution of the South." Just let one individual anywhere surrender "his inalienable rights of reason and conscience," his ability, that is, to know and willingness to do the right, and you will have a slavery worse than politics can devise.[16]

Social freedom, thought Thoreau, is less well understood even than political freedom. It is nothing less than "a freedom proportionate to the dignity" of a man's own nature (as he conceives this to be). It is a freedom "that shall make him feel that he is a man among men."[17] For Thoreau personally, this kind of freedom primarily meant—and demanded—the liberty to be oneself in the network of social speculations and expectations. He would teach himself because a socially accepted education "makes a straight-cut ditch of a free, meandering brook."[18] In the name of this freedom he would sever the ties that bind him to neighbors because he felt that his "connections with and obligations to society" were "very slight and transient."[19] Connections breed wants, wants breed connections, but freedom is solitary, want-free. He could rejoice that no one bought his books, the publisher's return of which was "more inspiring and better for me than if a thousand had bought my wares. It affects my privacy less and leaves me freer."[20] He could admire and set as a model his no-account friend, Bill Wheeler, "who went alone, did no work, had no relatives that I knew of, was not ambitious that I could see, and did not depend on the good opinion of men."[21] Even in heaven, that ultimate land of the free, he intended "to bake my own bread and clean my own linen," preferring—in the interest of social freedom as against communal servitude—to "keep bachelor's hall in hell than go to board in heaven."[22]

Thoreau's scorn for the commercial spirit, particularly as this takes the form of being "hired out" for a living, has already been remarked. However, it could also be noted that the commercial spirit (itself vulgar and vulgarizing) may result in a commercial slavery, even when one (like a farmer) works for himself. One is free, commercially, only when he labors for himself, in behalf of himself, and by himself. This freedom is the way to enjoyment. Thus, "I take some satisfaction in eating my food, as well as in being nourished by it. . . . I like best the bread which I have baked, the garment which I have made, the shelter which I have constructed, the fuel which I have gathered."[23] For all that they are self-employed, however, farmers generally are not free to enjoy the fruits of their own labor. Their land owns them; they do not own it. But, Thoreau wants to know, "Who made them serfs of the soil? Why should they eat their sixty acres, when man is condemned to eat only his peck of dirt?"[24] Or take the case of just one farmer, a certain Maynard, whose neat, orderly property Thoreau had admired. As if in wishful thinking, Maynard "had a tiger instead of a cock for a vane on his barn." Moreover, he looked "overworked," enjoying in his alleged freedom "only such content as an ox in his yard chewing cud."[25] He was a commercial slave.

Psychological freedom, finally, is a state of mind, an attitude. With it, even slaves are liberated. Without it, no man is truly free. It is a matter of "free and absolute thought" which transcends the merely "transitionary and paroxysmal."[26] It is freedom to "deal with truths that recommend themselves to me, please me, not merely those which any system has voted to accept"—a "meteorological journal of the mind" which is well beyond the "network of speculations," suggesting and offering the priceless, well-fortified right you have to observe "what occurs in your latitude, I in mine."[27] Such a freedom is taught by nature. You may read the lesson in a fireplace. "What an uncertain and negative thing" a flame is, says Thoreau, "when it finds nothing to suit its appetite after the first flash. What a positive and inexpugnable thing, when it begins to devour the solid wood with a relish, burning with its own wind."[28] In other words, a fire is miserable when it is constrained, grand when free to follow its own course. So also for man. You may read it in the free, uninhibited progress of rivers, living naturally, living freely, defying men and their history: "Thus in the course of ages the rivers wriggle in their beds till it feels comfortable under them. Time is cheap and rather insignificant. It matters not whether it is a river which changes from side to side in a geological period or an eel that wriggles past in an instant."[29] Freedom matters, nothing else. You may read it even in an encounter with a stray pig. He will have something to tell you about the origin of psychological freedom—and its great goal:

But really he is no more obstinate than I. I cannot but respect his tactics and his independence. He will be he, and I may be I. He is not unreasonable because he thwarts me, but only the more reasonable. He has a strong will. He stands upon his idea.[30]

To be psychologically free is "to live free"—free as "children of the mist."[31] Free of the network of speculations. Free politically and socially and commercially. Free in the mind, free as the mist itself, we can never settle for slavery of any sort. With such freedom, with that conviction of freedom, we can give the lie to necessity itself, and say No to demand:

> Must we still eat
> The bread we have spurned?
> Must we re-kindle
> The faggots we've burned?[32]

Simplicity

An utterly free man, Thoreau was also a very simple one. And if solitude was his ultimate in freedom, sincerity was the chief characteristic of his simplicity.

Out of his sincerity, with due regard for the facts that he was considered a savage and that he himself admired savages, he suggested and put forth "two kinds of simplicity,—one that is akin to foolishness, the other to wisdom." Whereas the savage lives "simply through ignorance, idleness, or laziness," the "philosopher lives simply through wisdom."[33] As a philosopher, then, not as a savage, he would present a philosophy of simplicity. This is the wisdom of being simple, of living simply.

Basic to this philosophy is both the connection with and the distinction from poverty. "What you call bareness and poverty," he declared, "is to me simplicity. God could not be unkind to me if he should try. It is the greatest of all advantages to enjoy no advantages at all."[34] The kind of poverty he recognized is a "simpler and truer relation to nature, gives a peculiar relish to life, just as to be kept short gives us an appetite for food."[35] It should be seen, in the main, as "simplicity of life and fewness of incidents." Through it one deliberately chooses a poorness of body in order to enjoy richness of spirit. What it does is to solidify or crystallize a man, "as a vapor or liquid by cold," making him chaste, giving him "a perpetual acquaintance with the All" thereby.[36]

To embrace such a philosophy, call it poverty or call

it simplicity, is (from Thoreau's point of view) to gain rather than to lose. That is its good sense. Thus for him to avow that "my greatest skill . . . has been to want but little"[37] is a declaration of strength, not a confession of weakness. Moreover, since he was convinced "both by faith and experience that to maintain one's self on this earth is not a hardship but a pastime—if we will live simply and wisely,"[38] the philosophy of simplicity (or poverty) which he proposes should be interpreted as something much more positive than negative. Life was a joy to him. Simplicity was his approach to joy.

The way to simplicity, however, led through, must lead through, the various built-in complexities and man-complicated factors of modern life. These had to be identified, then discarded or shunned. Take the matter of clothing, for example. If "one thick garment will suffice for three thin ones," then man "compounds" himself—and his needs—by wearing more than is necessary.[39] Rather, he should be clad so simply that "he can lay his hands on himself in the dark," indeed that "he live in all respects so compactly and preparedly that, if an enemy take the town, he can walk out the gate empty-handed without anxiety."[40] If this seems like a paraphrase of the "lilies-of-the-field" parable in the Bible, it may well be. It is also an attack on all possessions, both material and personal. For, as he put it, "Do not trouble yourself much to get new things, whether clothes or friends. Turn the old; return to them. Things do not change; we change. Sell your clothes and keep your thoughts."[41] In the same vein he tells us that "it is foolish for a man to accumulate material wealth chiefly, houses and land. Our stock in life is that amount of thought which we have had."[42] Just one unnecessary item may complicate our lives and negate our pure thought. Thus when a lady once offered Thoreau a mat to put before the door of his Walden hut, he declined to accept it on the grounds that "it is best to avoid the beginnings of evil."[43] For it is in apparently little matters that "men invite the devil in at every angle and then prate about the garden of Eden and the fall of man."[44] Too much of anything, even of a good such as fruit or plain water, much less of objects that we do not need or want, is "fatal to the morning's clarity."[45] In order to have pure thoughts, "a man's body must be rasped down exactly to a shaving. It is of far more importance than the wood of a Cremona violin."[46] Real simplicity, then, demands the rejection of anything or any action (even any person) which puts demands on us and thus decreases our capacity for the attentive enjoyment of essential living:

> If I buy one necessary of life, I cheat myself to some extent. I deprive myself of the pleasure, the inexpressible joy which is the unfailing reward of satisfying any want of our nature simply and truly. . . . No trade is simple, but artificial and complex. It postpones life and substitutes death. It goes against the grain.[47]

But if all man-made things (objects, trades, institutions) go against the grain, everything in nature exactly complements man's nature. In fact, the primary reason for ridding one's life of artificial complexities is to make it responsive to natural simplicity. A man would be insane, Thoreau said, to communicate with the gods (which is where natural simplicity directs our thoughts) if he is content to be "a pencil-maker on earth."[48] What he should concern himself with is "God's cheap economy," which will make him wealthy (in poverty) as well as wise (in innocent ignorance).[49] He should see all things as if by moonlight. For "by moonlight all is simple. We are enabled to erect ourselves, our minds, on account of the fewness of objects. We are no longer distracted. It is as simple as bread and water."[50] He should become "pliant and ductile" to nature's "strange but memorable influences," yielding himself to the "elemental tenderness" of earth."[51] He should "leave trifles to accident, and politics, and finance, and gossip."[52] He should conduct his affairs, all told, in such an essential, meaningful way (that is, pared down) that each rising and setting of the sun will find him fully prepared for, rather than indifferent to, what really counts. And so, "If the day and the night are such that you greet them with joy, and life emits a fragrance like flowers and sweet-scented herbs, is more elastic, more starry, more immortal,—that is your success."[53] Finally, he should live so simply that the rewards of simplicity will be self-evident—and even future hope, not to speak of past desires, will be less important to him than the unadorned, perfectly simple here and now. Thoreau suggests this kind of life:

> I wish so to live ever as to derive my satisfactions and inspirations from the commonest events, everyday phenomena, so that what my senses hourly perceive, my daily walk, the conversation of my neighbors, may inspire me—and I may dream of no heaven but that which lies about me.[54]

It was thus that Thoreau was able to extricate himself from the "network of speculations." In so doing he made small demands on himself, great demands on life. It did not take much to please him, nor did he think that successful simplicity required much more of him than "to be able to state a fact simply and adequately, to digest some experience clearly, to say yes and no with authority, to make a square edge."[55] But because what came naturally to him seemed very difficult to most men, he was at pains to set forth his doctrine of simplicity as explicitly as possible. He felt that most men, trapped by the network of complexity, were by the same token ignorant of how to escape. Therefore, he would "omit one bridge over the river, go round a little there, and throw one arch at least over the darkening gulf of ignorance which surrounds us."[56] More specifically, in two extended treatments of the subject of simplicity, he composed certain commandments (as it were)—the do's and don't's which would manifest the light and confound the ignorance.

In the famous *Walden* chapter called "Economy," borrowing that term from business and government, he set the life of the savage against that of the modern sophisticate, arguing that to be plainly clothed, simply housed, and elementally fed did not mean cheap living but rich living, whereas the complexities of modern society (overeating, finery, luxurious homes, compelling labors, the compulsion to improvement, intricacies of trade, the sop of philanthropy, the enervation of gentility) meant not the rich, full life but a cheap, deprived existence. If the rest of *Walden* demonstrated that it was possible to live well by living simply, the theory of simplicity itself is nobly enunciated in "Economy," a term whose root meaning is household management. Having set his own house in order, he felt entitled to advise on the subject.

This advice he also put in the form of an extended journal entry which looks very much like the decalogue of the life simple.[57] These are his prescriptions and prohibitions, with only the barest necessity of additional commentary:

1. Do what needs to be done. (Anything else becomes an encumbrance.)
2. Abolish thoughts of success or failure. (Be your own judge of your own contentment.)
3. "Dispose of evil. Get punished once and for all." (Guilt feelings, always socially inspired, are a luxury.)
4. "Die, if you can. Depart." (That is, act seriously, finally, not frivolously.)
5. Run necessary risks. (The only chance to take is with life itself.)
6. "If you can drive a nail and have any nails to drive, drive them." (There is honor enough in doing what lies next to you.)
7. Eat only when hungry. (Your body is the temple of the spirit, not a dumping-ground.)
8. Read no newspapers. (All the news you can possibly want is happening, has happened, in your own garden.)
9. Live with confidence. (Personal sincerity is the sole criterion of right and wrong.)
10. "Do what nobody can do for you. Omit to do

everything else." (Avoid foreign entanglements, in other words—and invisible networks.)

This simple, economical life: why is it so necessary? Because there is so little real life available—"the mere fragrance, rumor, and reminiscence" are all that we get. Therefore, when a good thought or an interesting experience comes along, "chew that cud . . . as long as there is any flavor in it." Keep on chewing, until "your keepers shake down some fresh fodder."[58] Old age will come soon enough. Will you be "serene and contented"? Then you must not yield, today, to "confusion and turmoil."[59] Will you, then and now, find the essentials of life? If so, you must declare the simplicity of self-reliance, the self-reliance of simplicity. For it is a fact that "all enterprises must be self-supporting, must pay for themselves. The great art of life is how to turn the surplus life of the soul into life for the body."[60]

Whereas, then, Etzler had proposed a mechanical means to paradise, Thoreau asserted that man needs only the rather more natural instrumentations of his own virtues to reform the world and to regain Adam's paradise. With the freedom that guarantees and is guaranteed by solitude, and with the simplicity that only a sincere man dares assay, one has paradise enough. Heaven is not a heartbeat away. It is this breath, and the next.

In fact, these virtues alone will qualify man for the touch of the infinite. At the very least they will declare him a religious person. And since all that Thoreau has been saying, under whatever heading, is basically religious, it remains only to be shown how he defined the nature of the religion he practiced and outlined the shape of the ecstasy this religion promised.

Chapter 9

A TOUCH OF THE INFINITE:
"SOME CLEAR, DIVINE ELECTUARY"

What is religion? That which is never spoken.[1]

There are secret articles in our treaties with the gods, of more importance than all the rest, which the historians can never know.[2]

Religion and allied subjects (such as conscience, morality, virtue, church establishment) figure prominently in Thoreau's formally published writings and more private journal meditations. In addition, he had a way of converting most other topics into ultimately religious ones, or at least of treating them from a religious point of view. Even when he seemed irreverent, moreover, he was never irreligious, there being always a sublime purpose to his iconoclasm.

Of course, as a man of religion he had no pulpit. In fact, he had no church. One supposes, on the basis of his direct and indirect references to the Bible, that he had a profound interest in, if not attachment to, the Christian religion, although so opposed was he to sectarianism that his Christianity (like Bonhoeffer's a century later) was quite religionless. Then, too, one cannot help but notice the way in which he set the unstructured, nature-based, asceticism-tending forms of Eastern beliefs over and against the more traditional Western beliefs.

To complicate the matter further, Thoreau confounds us with contradictions. For example, as a monk without a monastery, he lived sparingly, prayerfully, but attentive far more to this life than to the next. He was a transcendentalist, and yet quite unwilling to go where pure idealism should lead him—away from the real life really lived.

He preached joy. But is there not some Calvinistic gloom in it, not to speak of doctrines very much like those of natural depravity, salvation for the few only, and a kind of predestination? Finally, he saw the connection between moral excellence and formal religious institutes. However, he was likely to reverse the usual interpretation of that connection by claiming that religion, far from being a source of moral excellence, was actually a hindrance to it; and that, therefore, the rejection of religion is the first step toward the attainment of moral excellence.

In all, Thoreau's religion and religious attitudes were filled with love–hate inconsistencies, with perhaps the sole stable, stabilizing element in them his naturalism. For him nature was a metaphor of morals, his writing a metaphor of nature. We may not be able satisfactorily to classify Thoreau's beliefs of a religious sort, but at least we should begin with the understanding of the primacy of religious sentiment among his other notions, and of the fundamentalism of nature to this sentiment.

To begin to understand these things we should consider a text which he first mentioned in 1841, then introduced and anthologized in 1843, and to which—now obliquely, now frontally—he would return many times in the long, devious course of his religious speculations. We may take it that this text fairly well summarizes his early religious thought, and that it is an implication-filled introduction to his more maturely sublime thought.

As dissatisfied as Emerson was with standard Concord faiths and ministries, Thoreau turned to the Orient for some suitable substitute, although not primarily to the *Bhagavad Gita* (the standard scripture for the nonstandard). Instead he discovered and made his own the doctrine of Menu, son or grandson of Brahma, whose one hundred thousand verses, "promulgated in the beginning of time," transmit essentially and poetically the code of life set forth by Brahma, the God of gods, the Religion of religions. A first reading of this doctrine impressed him very much: "The sublime sentences of Menu carry us back to a time when purification and sacrifice and self-devotion had a place in the faith of men."[3] In fact, so impressed was he and so anxious to share his satisfaction with those whom orthodoxy dissatisfied, that he prepared an edition (abridged, retranslated, and somewhat transmuted) of that Indian classic, *The Laws of Menu*.[4] This edition is as much Thoreau as it is Menu—by both adaptation and adoption.

Under the headings of Custom, Temperance, Purification, Sacrifice, Teaching, Reward, Punishment, The King, Women and Marriage, The Brahmans, God, and Devotion, Thoreau says that Menu says that Brahma says that "immemorial custom may not be distinguished from revelation"; that "the resignation of pleasure is better than the attainment"; and that, when breath is sacrificed in speech (a man praying aloud) and speech is sacrificed in breath (a man meditating in silence), what is gained is "the imperishable fruit of a sacrificial offering." These sayings Thoreau could accept as pith and poetry.

Menu also says, we are told, that as grass is good for sitting and water for washing, so also "affectionate speech is at no time deficient in the mansions of the good"; that although Brahmans must sometimes perform menial tasks, they are always to be honored because they are "transcendentally divine"; that, if a man must work, he should "avoid service for hire"; and that, just as the good man should "shun worldly honor as he would shun poison," so must he "seek disrespect as he would seek nectar." Thoreau could well accept these sayings as tenets for his code of conduct.

But it is when Menu gets to certain more sublime considerations that Thoreau begins to perceive the nature of the true religion. This has three aspects: the individual soul, the quest for what Emerson had called Over Soul, and good counsel for the perfect life.

Of necessity the soul is single and singular. It is "its own refuge," "its own witness." Better to offend men than to offend it. Better still, let it become "the internal witness of men." Let this soul (called "conscious") cling to itself: "Alone, in some solitary place, let him constantly meditate on the divine nature of the soul; for, by such meditation, he will attain happiness."

The Over Soul is immanent as well as transcendent. It is to be found in all beings, and "all beings are to be found in it." One must sacrifice one's own spirit "by fixing it on the spirit of God." Indeed, one "approaches the nature of that sole divinity who shines by his only effulgence" via the soul of the self, not the selfishness of the soul.

As for the counsel to and from one who has penetrated the secret of soul and Soul, the prescriptions are very simple but very demanding. First, "Let every Brahman, with fixed attention, consider all nature both visible and invisible as existing in the divine spirit." Thus are all things holy, everything (willy-nilly) religious. Thus, too, is nature the one sure path to sublimity. Second, let every Brahman, "departing from his house, taking with him pure implements, his waterpot and staff, keeping silence, unallured by desire of objects," walk straight the narrow path. To what? To the one pure life in the midst of many impure, to the heaven on earth, to the fulfillment of human purposes by divine ways. Third, let every Brahman finally realize that his aspirations involve, require, terrible risks. Faith (here called devotion) will alone sustain him, making a solitary journey more than merely a lonely one:

> Whatever is hard to be traversed; whatever is hard to be acquired; whatever is hard to be visited; whatever is hard to be performed: all this may be accomplished by true devotion; for the difficulty of devotion is the greatest of all.[5]

Now, it may be argued, Thoreau took a circumlocutious route to get back where he started. God is Brahma. The "Laws" are a fanciful, Orientalized Bible. The code, at its highest level, is the saying of any saint; at its lowest, it is *Poor Richard's Almanac* in religious garb. The doctrine of renunciation had been preached better by Christ. Soul is soul in any religion. Over Soul is simply a metaphor. Devotion is faith. All this may be argued well and truly.

But the argument would be beside the point; beside three points, in fact: that, although the way was roundabout, it was Thoreau's way; that while the Hebraic-Christian tradition did uphold many of the same doctrines, it was enunciating them (at least to a nineteenth-century skeptic) in a flat, tired, prosaic, church-encumbered manner; and that the use of nature in and the ultimate *mysterium* of religion are weird exceptions in the West but marvelous commonplaces in the East.

At any rate, as we consider the religious message of Thoreau, we should realize and appreciate the naturalness of it—in the sense of its lack of artificiality, in the sense that it devolved quite simply and directly from nature, and in the sense that it quite satisfied his own nature. The topics he takes up under a religious heading (the use and abuse of religion; the sources of morality; God and beyond God; and, finally, mysticism under the title of Silence) are fairly standard. It is the approach to them that carries Thoreau's personal mark.

The Use and Abuse of Religion

In discussing his own brand of religion Thoreau tended to speak facetiously. He called himself a worshiper of "Hebe, the daughter of Juno and wild lettuce, who had the power of restoring gods and men to the vigor of youth."[6] So sterile was Concord's religion at the time, so spiritually impotent its preachers and practitioners, that he could do worse than opt for vitality, even if this was pagan. The only other alternative to hypocrisy (his name for contemporary worship) would be "to buy a share in the first Immediate Annihilation Company," an agency of his own devising which would put an end to spiritual values even faster than routine religion could.[7] He might just as well speak facetiously. When he was serious, few men understood him anyway. Occasionally, he tells us, he would address lyceum audiences on the subject of his beliefs, doing his "best to make a clean breast of what religion I have experienced." But, as often as not, "the audience never suspected what I was about.

The lecture was as harmless as moonshine to them."[8] Then there would be those who tried to realize his Walden experiment as the withdrawal of a religious fanatic to the desert, wondering what really sustained his ascetic life. Could it have been "vegetable food alone"? To these he responded thus: "To strike at the root of the matter at once,—for the root is faith,—I am accustomed to answer . . . that I live on board nails. If they cannot understand that, they cannot understand much that I have to say."[9] In a word, faith could sustain him. This they would not understand, in part because they had no faith, in part because their interpretation of faith was narrow and narrowing. Thoreau, on the other hand, identified "various, nay, incredible faiths. Why should we be alarmed at any of them? What a man believes, God believes."[10]

What this one man believed, however, whether or not God would ratify his faith, evidently came to slow fruition out of the careful study of many religions. In general, those of the ancient East appealed to him more than the religion of the Hebrews, his own spiritual ancestors. The idealistic Hindus and the aesthetic Sufis (if not the more practical, family-centered Confucians), for example, seemed to him to be more serenely and thoughtfully religious, as having attained through a purer, more independent, and less personal knowledge what might be termed a contemplative access to God.[11] At least they were not so guilt-ridden as the Hebrews, so that they were able to realize more joy in life out of their religion.

About Christianity Thoreau was somewhat ambivalent. Of the New Testament he could say: "I love this book rarely, though it is a sort of castle in the air to me, which I am permitted to dream." On the other hand, if read literally, it suited Thoreau's practical, uncomplacent nature. As he put the matter:

There are, indeed, several things in it which no man should read aloud more than once. "Seek first the kingdom of heaven." "Lay not up for yourselves treasures on earth." . . . Think of this, Yankees! Think of repeating these things to a New England audience.[12]

But there was a flaw in the book which made it, as a source of religion, unacceptable to Thoreau. This was that "it treats of man and man's so-called spiritual affairs too exclusively, and is too constantly moral and personal, to alone content me who am not interested solely in man's religious or moral nature, or in man even."[13] This flaw, moreover, seemed to stem from Christ himself, who "taught mankind but imperfectly how to live; his thoughts were all directed toward another world. There is another kind of success than his." Given our kind of life, more real than ideal, we must rather more than Christ advised "make shift to live, betwixt spirit and matter, such a human life as we can."[14]

If Christianity at its pure source failed to satisfy Thoreau because it was too other-worldly, the practicing Christians of his day and town disgusted him by their worldliness. He called them "the effete, gone to seed in a drought, mere human galls stung by the Devil once," whose idea of "joy and serenity" through religion is simply "reduced to grinning it and bearing it."[15] He said that their religion was "for the most part offensive to the nostrils," like "foul sores" which ought to be covered rather than exposed. Indeed, he said, "There is more religion in men's science than there is science in their religion. Let us make haste to the report of the committee on swine."[16] They think that they declare great truths in their excitingly new and liberal magazines of religious opinion, but not one (thought Thoreau) "dares say what it thinks about the Sunday or the Bible. They have been bribed to keep dark. They are in the service of hypocrisy."[17] They content themselves with and congratulate themselves on their artificial monuments to religion but always to the destruction of a nature sufficient to sustain them and worthy of their highest sentiments. "Let men tread gently through nature," said Thoreau. "Let us religiously burn stumps and worship in groves, while Christian vandals lay waste the forest temples to build miles of meeting-houses and horse-sheds, and feed their box stoves."[18] Finally, with their (to Thoreau) completely arbitrary and foolish codes of conduct derived from religion distantly and by now weakly, they even interfere with the course of nature. He noted, for example, that when the factories and mills closed down for Sunday, the upstream sluice gates would be shut. Let them go to church, if they must, thought Thoreau, but let them not ruin the naturalness of nature: "So completely emasculated and demoralized is our river that it is even made to observe the Christian sabbath, so that the very fishes feel the influence (or lack of influence) of man's religion."[19] They could influence fish, these men of religion, but not Thoreau. And although he had no love lost for innkeepers, he was willing to set their belief off against that of the religionists:

> Who ever thought of the religion of an innkeeper? But he keeps an inn and not a conscience. The church is the place where prayers and sermons are delivered, but the tavern is where they are to take effect, and if the former are good, the latter cannot be bad.[20]

The fact is, however, that it is the elders and saints who keep the inns going. Therefore, what price prayers and sermons?

With such views of religion, Thoreau surprises us that he saw any use in religion at all. What he objected to was the complexity, the artificiality, the excessive moralizing, the insufficient attention to nature, the hypocrisy, and the lack of joy and vitality in religion and his contemporary religionists. What he looked for was something simple, natural, glad, ideal (in the sense of urging a goal beyond one's grasp) but very real (that is, rooted in the soil of both physical and human nature). What he expected such a religion to do for him, should he ever find it, would be two things. One, it should help him better himself. He must keep his nature but he must also improve it. "Human nature," he said, "is hard to be overcome, but she must be overcome. What avails it that you are a Christian if you are not purer than the heathen, if you deny yourself no more, if you are not more religious?"[21] Two, true religion (or a true sense of religion) ought to supply that part of our nature which aspires to an "other" and "higher" nature. Indeed, he concluded, "the principle which prompts us to pay our involuntary homage to the infinite, the incomprehensible, the sublime" is the very basis of religion, the reason for its being.[22]

Sources of Morality

If what Thoreau says is true, that "the truly noble and settled character of a man is not put forward, as the king or emperor does not march foremost in a procession,"[23] we may be able to say in just what his morality consists. In fact, we are immediately struck by the seeming contradictions to be found in his several discussions of morality itself. He reminds us "how wonderfully moral [is] our whole life," how "wonderfully and admirably moral," with never "an instant's truce between virtue and vice."[24] He tells us, presumably also in admiration, that virtue (is it the cause or effect of morality?) is the "deed of the bravest, . . . an art which demands the greatest confidence and fearlessness."[25] Similarly but much more sweepingly, he asserts that "virtue is incalculable, as it is inestimable. Well, man's destiny is but virtue, or manhood. It is wholly moral, to be learned only by the life of the soul."[26] On the other hand, he evidently felt that there could be too much of even this good thing. He said that "what offends me most in my compositions is the moral element in them."[27] He complained that he had never met a man "who cast a free and healthy glance over life, but the best live in a sort of sabbath light, a Jewish gloom. The best thought is not only without somberness but even without morality. The moral aspect of nature is a jaundice reflected by man."[28] And he wondered why we "always insist that men incline to the moral side of their being. Our life is not all moral."[29]

Now he was certainly not making a declaration of immorality. Rather, in ridding morality of its usual connotations and associations, he was striving for a state or quality more natural, more interior, more fundamentally human and at the same time more preterhuman. He felt that men had routinized this free subject, taken too mechanical a view of it. But, he says, "It matters not what the clocks say or the attitudes and labors of men. Morning is when I am awake and there is a dawn in me. Moral reform is the effort to throw off sleep."[30] He also felt that men too quickly settled for too little in their pursuit of the essence of morality, that "the purity men love is like the mists which envelop the earth, and not the azure ether beyond."[31] He felt that, not despite but because of their rules and regulations governing moral behavior, men tended to confuse right (the original right) and wrong over the years, especially when they put forth the social over the personal conception of these values. Therefore, it could happen that "the greater part of what my neighbors call good I believe in my soul to be bad, and if I repent of any thing, it is . . . my good behavior."[32] Nor was he simply perverse when he said this. After all, man's criterion for conduct is conscience. But conscience (socially interpreted and restricted, not to say invented) has grown stale and tired. It is nothing more than

> . . . instinct bred in the house.
> Feeling and thinking propagate the sin
> By an unnatural breeding in and in.
> I say, turn it out doors,
> Into the moors.[33]

No, Thoreau's notion of morality is not licentious. It is, however, considerably more esoteric. Other men's notions would not do for him—simply because they were other men's. He recognized "continents and seas in the moral world to which every man is an isthmus or an inlet";[34] therefore man is susceptible to moral influences, even capable of the highest morality, but in an isolated way. He looked for "a universal innocence," not a set of prohibitions, one in which "poison is not poisonous after all, nor any wounds fatal."[35] He urged the kind of morality which nature, not men, would approve. Behave, he said, so that "the odor of your actions may enhance the general sweetness of the atmosphere, that, when I behold or scent a flower, I may not be reminded how inconsistent are your actions with it; for all odor is but one form of advertisement of a moral quality."[36] He related the moral character of a man to "a life of deep experiences,"[37] not to the superficial, external aids which, most men say, instruct or shape character. And he definitely saw morality as somehow related to something permanent in life, not a historical and surely not a contemporary mode of living. Therefore, he said, "Fix not thy heart on that which is transitory; for the Dijlah, or Tigris, will continue to flow through Bagdad after the race of caliphs is extinct; if thy hand has plenty, be liberal as the date tree; but if it affords nothing to give away, be an azad, or free man, like the cypress."[38]

Esoteric (by contrast with common opinion) as this notion of morality may be, it is no more strictly—or only—private than it is licentious. Thoreau, at any rate, speaks to his audience as if he not only had discovered the source of morality but had been charged with the responsibility of leading men to it. If it is fundamental to the life of a man, it follows that it can be known even if it is "uncommon." Why, then, do men deliberately choose the "common mode"? It is because "they honestly think there is no choice left. But alert and healthy natures remember that the sun rose clear. It is never too late to give up our prejudices."[39] He would assist them in the arduous process of giving up their prejudices about the moral life by reminding them of four uncommon precepts of morality. The precepts are abstract, but their practice may be particular and concrete. Whether one proceeds from the general to the particular or from the particular to the general, he should discover (Thoreau thought) an indivisible morality. First, he said, we should know that nature is our first and greatest teacher of morals. It is from her that we should learn to make the distinctions that are so basic to the moral life. In her plan "the humblest, puniest weed that can endure the sun is superior to the largest fungus. All things flower, both vices and virtues, but the one is essentially foul, the other fair."[40] Second, in the divine plan for human beings, not only our treatment of divinity but our recognition of it in each man (our fellow mortal) are essential to morality. We should realize, then, that "nearest to all things is that power which fashions their being. Next to us the grandest laws are continually being executed. Next to us is not the workman whom we have hired . . . but the workman whose work we are."[41] Third, however we may define morality, we must be able to note its effects on our character. We are all rational animals; we all see our highest virtue in intelligence, in our ability to compose and to grasp pure thought. But, Thoreau said, "How can we expect a harvest of thought who have not had a seed-time of character?"[42] Fourth, we may take it that the thrust of all morality, of all moral acts, is toward purity of soul. And yet, since this is hardly understood, much less readily attained, our approach to it must be indirect, by way of steps which may be understood and simply taken. As he put the matter:

If you would be chaste, you must be temperate. What is chastity? How shall a man know if he is chaste? He shall not know it. We have heard of this virtue, but we know not what it is. We speak comfortably to the rumor we have heard.[43]

God and Beyond God

There is some connection between Thoreau's God and his religion—but not as much as one might ordinarily expect to find. The two may be related, but not necessarily. Similarly, there could be a connection between Thoreau's notion of what God stands for and the requirement that man be moral. Again, however, just as it is possible to have a godless religion or a God who is beyond the reach of religion, so also is it possible for Thoreau to conceive of a human and suprahuman moral system which is separate and distinct.

If God is an ultimate being, Thoreau is much more comfortable in dealing with a proximate being. He admired "Chaucer's familiar, but innocent, way of speaking of God."[44] And one time, spelling the term with a small "g," he congratulated himself—not for his temerity but for his simple, natural affection, claiming that he "had brought in the word without any solemnity of voice or connection."[45] When he gave thanks to this God, it was not for grand or grandiose gestures on God's part but for the kind of cheery, familiar, friendly, one might almost say domestic acts that a fellow mortal (rustic and earthy, too) could appreciate. Thus, he said, "Ah, bless the Lord, O my soul! bless him for wildness, for crows that will not alight within gunshot! and bless him for hens, too, that croak and cackle in the yard."[46] He gave this God a place in the universe, that is true, but he also put Him in His place by cutting down on the demands He might legitimately make on men, or those that men think He makes. It would appear, he thought, that man is "in a strange uncertainty about life, whether it is of the devil or of God, and *somewhat hastily* concluded that it is the chief end of men here 'to glorify God and enjoy him forever.' "[47] (Thoreau, of course, felt that there was much more to life, and automatically reduced the relationship of man to God.) Finally, while recognizing the sublime and ultimate aspects of God, he refused the notion of the mysterious, aloof *"deus absconditus."* Instead he will accept the reality of God, known and knowable, in the reality of man and man's world, known and knowable. And so he said:

In eternity there is indeed something true and sublime. But all these times and places and occasions are now and here. God himself culminates in the present moment, and will never be more divine in the lapse of all the ages. We are enabled to apprehend at all what is sublime and noble only by the perpetual instilling and drenching of the reality that surrounds us.[48]

To a certain extent, then, we might say, Thoreau minimizes God, granting Him some uniqueness, some power, but not much majesty, not much mystery, at the same time insisting that he or any other man should be respected for his uniqueness, his power, and whatever small amounts of majesty and mystery he might have. God is not over there. He is here, along with men.

At the same time, however, Thoreau had a way of talking about "an unsought, unseen, . . . clear, divine electuary" which seems to be beyond both men and God, and which is capable of turning a merely "sensual" creature into a "sensible" one.[49] Other men might quibble about this phenomenon, maintaining that it is God. But Thoreau saw the matter differently—and chose his terms from a philosophical or mystical lexicon rather than from standard reference works in theology. He spoke, for example, of "a universal intelligence" which created nature, is in harmony with nature, and the traces of which can be found only in nature.[50] In still another place he words it slightly differently: "I see, smell, taste, hear, feel, that Everlasting Something to which we are called, at once our maker, our abode, our destiny, our very Selves."[51] Finally, we note that he employs the term "Spirit," usually in some kind of close relationship to nature (for example, nature is Spirit, Spirit is nature): "The strongest wind cannot stagger a Spirit; it is a Spirit's breath."[52]

Now it may be that Thoreau's circumlocutions were chosen specifically in order to avoid the associations usually attached to God in Concord (church establishment, for example). It may be that his notion of a Power beyond power is simply his way of asserting what the Greeks meant by making even the most potent gods subservient to *moira* or fate. It may be that he had absorbed just enough of a mixture of Platonic idealism and Oriental mysticism to speak familiarly, if disconcertingly, of pure thought, pure idea, pure ideal, as if he had been in contact with them. Or it may be that he wanted the god of nature (or whatever it was that made nature what it was) separate and distinct from all other gods, or conceptions of divinity.

Whatever the explanation, it would appear that the "electuary," god or no god, is divine, that the "sensible" (not the "sensual") man can comprehend it and correspond with it ("There are secret articles in our treaties . . . of more importance than all the rest, which the historians can never know"[53]), and that it speaks to man, indeed it beckons to him, out of the depths of nature.

Under the influence of the electuary, man can do without formal religion, without the usual codes of morality, and even without God or god. One such man, a hero to the author of *Walden,* was the legendary artist of Kouroo. He was disposed, Thoreau said, to "strive after perfection." (And, after all, isn't this what religion and morality and God are for?) Marching to other drums, however, and undoubtedly touched by the electuary (or something very much like it), he elected to find perfection, to be perfect, in the making of a staff. "Having considered that in an imperfect work time is an ingredient, but into a perfect work time does not enter, he said to himself, It shall be perfect in all respects, though I should do nothing else in my life." By the time he had chosen his stick, the city of Kouroo was in ruins. By the time he had shaped it, dynasties had fallen. And before he had finished it, Brahma himself "awoke and slumbered many times." But what he had accomplished was perfection itself, "the fairest of all creations." In making a staff, "he had made a new system, a world with full and fair proportions." He had, not quite incidentally, become immortal.

Now the secret of his success and the moral of the story have nothing to do with, say, obstinate individualism or persistent idealism. As Thoreau worded it, the moral was: "The material was pure, and his art was pure; how could the result be other than wonderful?"[54] As we might interpret this moral in the present context, however, our wording would be something like this: When a free, simple man responds naturally to the good in this world, he opens himself to the touch of the infinite, to the saving ministry of the divine electuary. When sensual, he needs religion and morality and God. When sensible, he needs nothing. He is perfect.

The Sound of Silence

Thoreau's story, really a parable on perfection, may seem to be merely poetry. But, as he reminds us, "In the last stage of civilization, Poetry, Religion, and Philosophy will be one; and this truth is glimpsed in the first."[55] Assuming, however, that we might want our religion and philosophy a little more straight (even if still somewhat mythical and mystical), Thoreau explains for us the marvelous state, or intuition of a state, which perfection discloses to us. It is the state of silence.

In commenting on the words used to describe the achievement of the Atlantic telegraph ("Glory to God in the highest"), he remarked that it "was not a sentiment to be illuminated, but to be kept dark about. I felt a kind of shame for it. What is religion? That which is never spoken."[56] In a more extended journal entry, he makes the same point, also suggesting that, whereas the imperfect hear only sound, the perfect hear Silence.[57]

What is Silence? It was "before even the world was." It is a "communing of a conscious soul with itself." It is "divine." It is "uttered to the inward ear" only, "bathing the temples of the soul." It is "an infinite expansion of our being" as well as "a universal refuge." Silence is "always at hand with her wisdom, by roadsides and street corners; lurking in belfries, the cannon's mouth, and the wake of the earthquake; gathering up and fondling their puny din in her ample bosom." He who through the perfection of his religious nature can hear Silence at last finds what all men seek: "Truth, Goodness, Beauty." For through Silence "have all revelations been made." Silence is indeed the ultimate.

Thoreau here seems to be fashioning a mystical state (one with the One, alone with the All). More likely, however, in that he was too much of a Yankee to be a good mystic, he is simply asserting a natural fact inspirationally phrased. At any rate, a silence beyond sound is no less or more understandable than a religionless religion, a morality above morality, a god beyond God. Its advantages are that it is simple, it is natural, it avoids the obvious, it is suggestive. Furthermore, it is everything that religion or morality or theology holds out to a man. But it is more poetic than any of these. And it is, finally, as close as one can come to an intuition (knowledge will not do) of the divine electuary.

What must be, then, the last word on the perfection to which all of Thoreau's thoughts on religion have been tending? It can only—and quite characteristically—be this:

As the truest society approaches always nearer to solitude, so the most excellent speech finally falls into Silence.[58]

AFTERWORD

The Leonard Baskin-designed postage stamp issued on July 12, 1967, to commemorate the Thoreau sesquicentennial, some note with approval and admiration, is appropriately simple, almost starkly severe in its elemental black-and-whiteness. Sharply angular to the first glance, it continues to arrest attention by the challenging tilt of the head, the piercing eyes, and the hard, harsh, rough texture of the face. A real man glares out between the name and the denomination, not without the hint of some affection but primarily with the look of a prophet bent on something much more serious and significant than kindliness.

At least a few Americans, on the other hand, have objected to the portrait not because it is not, in its own way, a good likeness but because the image does not reflect the qualities they expect to find in memorials of great men: gentleness (as against the toughness of this image), gentility (as against its wildness), classical dignity (this is very human, very contemporary), and aloof idealism (this is realistic, if not naturalistic). They seem to prefer, in their idols as in their art, that which is "safe," if not actually timid. But Baskin's Thoreau is dangerous, even capable of violence, and not a little mad.

Artistic merit and historical accuracy aside, however, it should be noted that both parties to the dispute have taken a subjective reading of this Concord pencil-maker become famous in spite of himself. Undoubtedly Thoreau would have appreciated subjectivity in a man's approach to him. After all, this is how he always approached his fellows. Not so certainly would he have approved the purely subjective, merely partial uses to which his life and work have been put, his name given, and his inspiration credited. Such oddly diverse and diversely odd groups as passive resisters, freedom marchers, states-righters, vegetarians, antivivisectionists, organic farmers, conservationists, Soho bohemians, and even Washington Square "hippies" have claimed him as their own, their very own. Whether he would have acknowledged them as sons and heirs is a different matter.

A private man, he did nevertheless teach a public lesson and preach a public gospel in the full expectation that he would be heard by different people for different reasons. Still, it is as general teacher and universal preacher, not as this or that propagandist, that he should be heard. And although he spoke to certain Americans in his own day, he has something to give everybody today.

Our question should be: What is Thoreau's use now?

As a teacher he had important things to say about consciousness. As a preacher he had significant things to say about conscience. His "use," therefore, may very well be resolved into these two vital areas of human concern.

That he spoke from personal conviction and positive confidence is quite clear. That the source of his message was not a rational philosophy so much as a real life well lived is equally definite:

> I would fain communicate the wealth of my life to men, would really give them what is most precious in my gift. I would secrete pearls with the shellfish and lay up honey with the bees for them. I will sift the sunbeams for the public good. I know no riches I would keep back. I have no private good, unless it be my peculiar ability to serve the public.[1]

His first service to any public in any age or circumstance is to make them aware: aware of the infinite possibility of life (his only subject, it turns out) as opposed to the unrealized potential of the lives most men lead. One supposes that, with Socrates, he agreed that the unexamined life is not worth living. But his message went beyond examination, his doctrine of consciousness reaching further than analysis, right into living itself. "See what a life the gods have given us," he said. It is "set round with pain and pleasure. It is too strange for sorrow; it is too strange for joy."[2] Examination and analysis turn up strangeness only. Living, on the other hand, is all you need to know of life, is sufficient for consciousness, and is the full meaning of awareness. It was not for Thoreau to contrive a philosophy but to live a life. By the same token, the public consciousness should be of the life, of the living, not of the philosophy.

The perennial virtues of his life may be most readily grasped by contrasts. He lived simply—to prove that "less is more." He lived quietly—to prove that gregariousness is the delusion of a sick society. He lived naturally—to prove the ultimate failure of machinery to touch the core of life. If we are adept at the efficient management of our business, he teaches the larger, more fundamental economy of life itself. If we bewail the fact that the physical frontiers are now closed to us, he teaches how we may keep open our spiritual borders. If we demand freedom, he teaches independence from all restraining institutions.

As he lived this life in demonstration of these contrasts, he was no Quixote tilting at windmills, no Miniver Cheevey sighing and weeping. Perhaps, like the former, he set the Age of Gold off against the Age of Iron. Perhaps, like the latter, he personally preferred armor to khaki, Camelot to Bridgeport. But preference is not the point here. His own experience, in support of the preference and against the common experience, is the point: the point of his own satisfied consciousness, the point of his lesson to the dissatisfied.

Even today his experience is still possible. Under the most adverse conditions it is possible. Imagine, if you will, a modern city-dweller, subway-riding, cafeteria-eating, overdressed, under-read, working on an assembly line, punching time clocks, forever caught up in a rat race, surrounded by gadgets, and institutionalized to an absurdity. Can such a one share the Thoreauvian experience? He not only can but he must. Well, then, can he have this experience without, let us say, living in a hut,

[152]

spending time in jail for tax delinquency, cutting his ties to all institutions (government, school, and church, to name three), giving up his friends, and (bred on the city streets, mind you) learning to track a muskrat? Most assuredly he can. The explanation is that Thoreau's doctrine of consciousness should not be understood in specifics and close particulars. What it offers is not a *quid pro quo* arrangement. Thus, when he teaches individualism, he means that you should mold your own, not imitate his. When he teaches the values of an interior, meditative life, he means these to apply to mobs on city streets, not merely to solitaries in forests or deserts. When he teaches the romantic ideals (intuition, imagination, feeling), he means them to apply, to apply most particularly, to very real, very sordid existences. When he opposes high seriousness to certain kinds of triviality, he means us to make our own distinctions between what is important and what is not. When he says that life is holy and men divine, he means all life (not just his), all men (our acquaintances as well as his). He teaches wildness: this is as applicable in the apartment complex as it is in the woods. He demands that nature be recognized: this can be done in an urban center as well as in Concord. When he says No to No and Yes to Yes, he does not preclude the possibility of any man in any circumstance saying yea to what is right, nay to what is wrong.

In short, it is our consciousness of his lessons that counts, not a memorization of the circumstances in his life which gave rise to them. It is the living of our own lives which matters, not the repetition of his. Consciousness, then, is *our* awareness of *our* duty to *our* life. Circumstances and conditions are not at issue. How Thoreau managed his affairs is not at issue. Furthermore, when he taught that "the whole duty of life is contained in the question how to respire and aspire both at once,"[3] he was asserting—out of private consciousness but in behalf of the public consciousness—that any life may be fully lived (respire) and at the same time be ideally motivated (aspire).

Such a consciousness begets, has to beget, a conscience. That is, once a man is made aware of the sacral nature of living, of the sacred possibilities of life, then he is forever committed, must be completely devoted, to the good life. Nothing less will do. Indeed, the life of his very soul is bound to this life. Therefore, Thoreau always joined conscience to consciousness. Therefore, too, in distinctly biblical terms, he gave a personalized, distinctively human, universally moral (that is, pertaining to the customs of men) answer to that most terrible question: What does it profit a man if he gains the whole world and suffers the loss of his soul?

Consciousness-based but conscience-directed, Thoreau's thought is single and simple: how to save one's soul. To the extent that this thought is accepted and acted upon, to that extent Thoreau has a use.

Finally, one should be reminded of the legendary bird which flies backward—because it does not care where it is going but likes to know where it has been. The careful student of Thoreau learns where he has been—in order to discover where he is going.

BIBLIOGRAPHY

The standard edition (called "Walden" or "Manuscript") of the *Writings of Henry David Thoreau* (Boston: Houghton Mifflin Company, 1906) comprises twenty volumes: I, *A Week on the Concord and Merrimack Rivers;* II, *Walden;* III, *The Maine Woods;* IV, *Cape Cod and Miscellanies;* V, *Excursions and Poems;* VI, *Familiar Letters;* and VII-XX, *Journal.* A newer edition of the last, used in the present work, has been published separately in fourteen volumes (New York: Dover Publications, Inc., 1963). Those seeking more scholarly editions of several of the titles in the complete works should consult, as was done here, *The Correspondence of Henry David Thoreau,* edited by Walter Harding and Carl Bode (New York: New York University Press, 1958); *The Collected Poems of Henry Thoreau,* edited by Carl Bode (Baltimore, Md.: The Johns Hopkins Press, 1964); *The Variorum Walden,* annotated and edited by Walter Harding (New York: Twayne Publishers, Inc., 1962); and *Consciousness in Concord: The Text of Thoreau's Hitherto Lost Journal, 1840–1841,* with Notes and Commentary by Perry Miller (Boston: Houghton Mifflin Company, 1958).

Two early biographies are still useful: *Henry D. Thoreau,* by F. B. Sanborn (Boston: Houghton Mifflin Company, 1882), and *The Life of Henry David Thoreau,* by Henry S. Salt (London: Walter Scott, 1896). The most recent purely factual biography is *The Days of Henry Thoreau,* by Walter Harding (New York: Alfred A. Knopf, Inc., 1965).

Biographical studies which are somewhat more appreciative and/or critical include, in the order of their publication, *Henry Thoreau: Bachelor of Nature,* by Leon

BIBLIOGRAPHY

Bazalgette (New York: Harcourt, Brace and World, Inc., 1924); *Henry Thoreau: The Cosmic Yankee*, by Brooks Atkinson (New York: Alfred A Knopf, Inc., 1927); *Thoreau*, by Henry Seidel Canby (Boston: Houghton Mifflin Company, 1939); *Henry David Thoreau*, by Joseph Wood Krutch (New York: William Sloane Associates, 1948); and *Henry David Thoreau: A Critical Study*, by Mark Van Doren (New York: Russell & Russell Publishers, 1961).

There are numerous purely critical works on Thoreau. Some of the best, modern in date and point of view, are the still-exciting interpretation in *The American Renaissance*, by F. O. Matthiessen (New York: Oxford University Press, Inc., 1941); *Walden Revisited*, by George F. Whicher (Chicago: Packard, 1945); *The Shores of America: Thoreau's Inward Exploration*, by Sherman Paul (Urbana, Ill.: University of Illinois Press, 1958); Perry Miller's provocative introduction to *Consciousness in Concord* (1958); *A Thoreau Handbook*, by Walter Harding (New York: New York University Press, 1959); and *Thoreau*, edited by Sherman Paul (Englewood Cliffs, N.J.: Prentice-Hall, Inc., 1965), a collection of essays by several hands.

For background material of a specialized sort (i.e., Thoreau's Eastern interests), the reader is directed to *The Orient in American Transcendentalism*, by Arthur Christy (New York: Columbia University Press, 1932). Finally, one can learn a great deal about Thoreau from his contemporaries. The most important references will be found in the *Journals* of Emerson and Bronson Alcott and the *American Notebooks* of Hawthorne.

NOTES

(*Legend:* The following abbreviations will be used throughout the Notes to refer to certain of the items listed in the Bibliography.)

W—*A Week* (Vol. I of *Writings*)
MW—*Maine Woods* (Vol. III)
CC—*Cape Cod* (Vol. IV)
E—*Excursions* (Vol. V)
FL—*Familiar Letters* (Vol. VI)
J—*Journal* (1963 edition)
C—*Correspondence* (Harding–Bode)
P—*Collected Poems* (Bode)
VW—*Variorum Walden* (Harding)
HS—Henry Salt's *Life of Henry David Thoreau*

Chapter 1

1. *J:* I, 347 (Mar. 25, 1842).
2. *C,* p. 67 (to Isaiah T. Williams, Mar. 14, 1842).
3. *The Service,* ed. by F. B. Sanborn (Boston: Goodspeed, 1902).
4. *Ibid.,* p. x.
5. *Ibid.,* p. 26.
6. *J:* VIII, 135 (Jan. 24, 1856).
7. *The Journals of Ralph Waldo Emerson,* ed. by E. W. Emerson and W. E. Forbes (Boston: Houghton Mifflin Company, 1912), Vol. VIII, p. 228.
8. *Ibid.,* IV, 397.
9. *W,* pp. xvii, xxviii (biographical sketch by Emerson).
10. *HS,* p. 90.
11. *J:* V, 58 (Mar. 28, 1853). This entry records a conversation between his aunts Maria and Jane.
12. *J:* V, 365 (Aug. 10, 1853).

13. *VW*, p. 14. The editor here cites a letter to Thoreau from Ellery Channing, dated Mar. 5, 1845.

14. *J:* XI, 380 (Dec. 27, 1858).

15. *J:* IV, 45 (May 9, 1852).

16. *J:* IX, 495 (July 29, 1857).

17. *C*, p. 279 (to T. W. Higginson, Apr. 2, 1852).

18. *Ibid.*, p. 120 (to Mrs. Emerson, June 20, 1843).

19. *J:* I, 350 (Mar. 26, 1842).

20. *J:* X, 115 (Oct. 21, 1857).

21. *J:* III, 222 (Jan. 24, 1852).

22. *J:* III, 311 (Feb. 18, 1852).

23. *J:* IX, 121 (Oct. 18, 1856).

24. *J:* X, 131 (Oct. 27, 1857).

25. *J:* II, 404–5 (Aug. 19, 1851).

26. *VW*, p. 74.

27. *Ibid.*, pp. 25–26, 34.

28. *Ibid.*, p. 93.

29. *C*, p. 436 (to Thomas Cholmondeley, Oct. 20, 1856).

30. *J:* XII, 371 (Oct. 4, 1859).

31. *VW*, p. 142.

32. *MW*, p. 59.

33. *W*, p. 21.

34. *J:* XII, 366–67 (Oct. 3, 1859).

35. *J:* III, 368 (Mar. 31, 1852).

36. *CC*, p. 353.

37. *J:* VI, 100 (Feb. 5, 1854).

38. *J:* VI, 165 (Mar. 12, 1854).

39. *J:* VI, 417 (Aug. 2, 1854).

40. *J:* XII, 31 (Mar. 10, 1859).

41. *CC*, pp. 297, 302, 304.

42. *C*, p. 384 (to H. G. O. Blake).

43. *J:* XIII, 226 (Mar. 25, 1860).

44. *VW*, p. 40.

45. *W*, p. 121.

46. *J:* XI, 275 (Nov. 1, 1858).

Chapter 2

1. *J:* I, 26 (Jan. 21, 1838).

2. *J:* I, 239 (Mar. 13, 1841).

3. *Sir Walter Raleigh*, introduced by F. B. Sanborn and edited by H. A. Metcalf (Boston: Bibliophile Society, 1905).

4. *Ibid.*, p. 40.
5. *Ibid.*, p. 68.
6. *Ibid.*, p. 83.
7. *VW*, p. 25.
8. *Ibid.*, p. 58.
9. *J:* V, 515 (Nov. 21, 1853).
10. *J:* II, 285 (July 6, 1851).
11. *J:* XII, 97 (Mar. 28, 1859).
12. *J:* VIII, 204–5 (Mar. 11, 1856).
13. *J:* I, 296 (Dec. 15, 1841).
14. *J:* I, 344 (Mar. 23, 1842).
15. *VW*, p. 123.
16. *J:* VI, 87 (Jan. 31, 1854).
17. *J:* II, 314 (July 16, 1851).
18. *C*, p. 407 (to Calvin Greene, Feb. 19, 1856).
19. *J:* III, 66 (Oct. 12, 1851).
20. *J:* IV, 417 (Nov. 23, 1852).
21. *J:* VII, 491 (Oct. 18, 1855).
22. *J:* VI, 452 (Aug. 18, 1854).
23. *MW*, p. 132.
24. *J:* IX, 145 (Dec. 1, 1856).
25. *J:* II, 306 (July 14, 1851).
26. *J:* I, 182 (Jan. 29, 1841).
27. *J:* II, 76 (Oct. 31, 1850).
28. *P*, p. 119.
29. *J:* I, 191 (Feb. 3, 1841).
30. *J:* I, 129 (Mar. 21, 1840).
31. *J:* I, 28 (Feb. 9, 1838).
32. *J:* I, 324 (Mar. 2, 1842).
33. *J:* I, 32–33 (Mar. 4, 1838).
34. *The American Notebooks* (Boston: Houghton Mifflin Company, 1891). Hawthorne's entry is dated Apr. 7, 1843.
35. *C*, p. 45 (to Mrs. Lucy Brown, July 21, 1841).
36. *J:* IX, 43 (Aug. 30, 1856).
37. *W*, p. 54.
38. *MW*, pp. 78–79.
39. *J:* VIII, 44 (Dec. 11, 1855).
40. *J:* V, 43 (Mar. 23, 1853).
41. *J:* XIII, 22 (Dec. 12, 1859).
42. *J:* IV, 218 (July 11, 1852).
43. *J:* I, 147 (June 21, 1840).
44. *J:* I, 384 (Aug. 23, 1845).
45. *VW*, p. 177.
46. *J:* I, 53–54 (Aug. 13, 1838).

47. *J:* II, 43–44 (July 16, 1850).
48. *J:* II, 267 (June 22, 1851).
49. *J:* II, 228 (June 6, 1851).
50. *C,* p. 52 (to Isaiah T. Williams, Sept. 8, 1841).
51. *J:* VIII, 115 (Jan. 18, 1856).
52. *J:* V, 75 (Mar. 30, 1853).
53. *J:* V, 45 (Mar. 5, 1853).
54. *CC,* p. 32.
55. *J:* XIII, 144 (Feb. 13, 1860).
56. *VW,* p. 124.
57. *J:* I, 380–81 (Aug., 1845). This passage describes his first visit to Walden Pond at the age of five.
58. *J:* X, 127 (Oct. 26, 1857).
59. *E,* p. 118.
60. *FL,* pp. 8–10. The address is cited in F. B. Sanborn's Introduction but is not given in its entirety.
61. *J:* II, 315 (July 18, 1851).
62. *J:* III, 372 (Apr. 1, 1852).
63. *J:* IX, 249–50 (Feb. 8, 1857).
64. *E,* pp. 105–6.
65. *HS,* p. 151. The author is quoting Thoreau at age seventeen.

Chapter 3

1. *J:* XII, 159 (Apr. 24, 1859).
2. *J:* III, 351 (Mar. 15, 1852).
3. *E,* pp. 205–48. First delivered as a lecture before the Concord Lyceum under the title of "The Wild " in 1851, it was altered and expanded during the last days of his life and published, posthumously, in *The Atlantic Monthly.*
4. *Ibid.,* p. 205.
5. *Ibid.,* p. 206.
6. *Ibid.,* pp. 245–46.
7. *J:* II, 101 (Nov. 16, 1850).
8. *J:* I, 299 (Dec. 25, 1841).
9. *J:* I, 152 (June 25, 1840).
10. *MW,* p. 58.
11. *Ibid.,* p. 87.
12. *W,* p. 138.
13. *J:* XI, 152 (Sept. 8, 1858).
14. *J:* I, 173 (Jan. 23, 1841).

15. *J:* XI, 304 (Nov. 9, 1858).
16. *J:* V, 16–17 (Mar. 12, 1853).
17. *J:* III, 184 (Jan. 12, 1852).
18. *J:* IV, 433 (Dec. 28, 1852).
19. *J:* I, 342 (Mar. 22, 1842).
20. *W,* p. 147.
21. *J:* IX, 36 (Aug. 30, 1856).
22. *J:* II, 390 (Aug. 15, 1851).
23. *VW,* p. 149.
24. *Ibid.,* p. 259.
25. *W,* p. 326.
26. *J:* XIII, 35 (Dec. 19, 1859).
27. *J:* XIII, 69 (Dec. 31, 1859).
28. *J:* XIV, 57 (Aug. 22, 1860).
29. *J:* V, 379 (Aug. 19, 1853).
30. *J:* VI, 294 (May 23, 1854).
31. *J:* IX, 151 (Dec. 3, 1856).
32. *J:* X, 191 (Nov. 20, 1857).
33. *J:* X, 258 (Jan. 25, 1858).
34. *C,* p. 313 (to H. G. O. Blake, Dec. 19, 1853).
35. *W,* p. 45.
36. *VW,* p. 255.
37. *J:* XII, 343 (Sept. 23, 1859).
38. *J:* IV, 15 (May 3, 1852).
39. *J:* XIV, 108 (Oct. 9, 1860).
40. *J:* I, 74 (Mar. 3, 1839).
41. *J:* II, 471 (Sept. 7, 1851).
42. *J:* VI, 43 (Jan. 1, 1854).
43. *J:* III, 99 (Nov. 8, 1851).
44. *C,* p. 330 (to H. G. O. Blake, Aug. 8, 1854).
45. *J:* III, 156–57 (Dec. 25, 1851).
46. *E,* p. 131.
47. *VW,* p. 33.
48. *J:* I, 9 (Nov. 12, 1837).
49. *J:* VIII, 134 (Jan. 24, 1856).
50. *FL,* pp. 8–10.
51. *J:* VIII, 181 (Feb. 14, 1856).
52. *J:* VI, 53 (Jan. 7, 1854).
53. *W,* p. 408.
54. *VW,* p. 78.
55. *C,* p. 257 (to H. G. O. Blake, Apr. 3, 1850).
56. *J:* III, 253 (Jan. 30, 1852).
57. *J:* II, 171 (Feb. 27, 1851).
58. *C,* p. 188 (to Emerson, Nov. 14, 1847).

59. *J:* V, 277 (June 18, 1853).

60. *Memories of a Sculptor's Wife,* by Mrs. Daniel Chester French (Boston, 1928), p. 95.

61. *J:* VI, 329 (June 5, 1854).

Chapter 4

1. *W,* pp. 136–37.
2. *J:* IV, 77 (May 30, 1852).
3. *E,* pp. 290–322. The essay was first published, posthumously, in *The Atlantic Monthly,* Nov., 1862.
4. *Ibid.,* pp. 295–96.
5. *Ibid.,* p. 307.
6. *Ibid.,* pp. 321–22.
7. *J:* I, 51 (June 16, 1838).
8. *J:* I, 174–75 (Jan. 24, 1841).
9. *J:* IX, 217 (Jan. 11, 1857).
10. *J:* I, 155 (June 29, 1840).
11. *J:* VI, 483 (Aug. 28, 1854).
12. *VW,* p. 88.
13. *Ibid.,* p. 28.
14. *J:* VIII, 229 (Mar. 26, 1856).
15. *J:* X, 6–7 (Aug. 10, 1857).
16. *W,* p. 136.
17. *J:* I, 39 (Mar. 14, 1838).
18. *J: IV,* 397 (Oct. 23, 1852).
19. *C,* p. 537 (to H. G. O. Blake, Jan. 1, 1859).
20. *Ibid.,* pp. 111–12 (to Emerson, June 8, 1843).
21. *J:* VI, 15 (Dec. 9, 1853).
22. *J:* V, 10 (Mar. 7, 1853).
23. *J:* XIII, 272 (May 2, 1860).
24. *J:* I, 36 (Mar. 14, 1838).
25. *J:* III, 194 (Jan. 16, 1852).
26. *J:* VIII, 7–8 (Nov. 5, 1855).
27. *W,* pp. 136–37.
28. *E,* p. 80.
29. *J:* XI, 324–26 (Nov. 16, 1858).
30. *J:* X, 351 (Apr. 3, 1858).
31. *J:* X, 344–45 (Apr. 2, 1858).
32. *J:* XII, 330 (Sept. 16, 1859).
33. *J:* II, 403–4 (Aug. 19, 1851).
34. *W,* p. 135.

35. *J:* II, 328 (July 21, 1851).
36. *J:* I, 426 (1845–1847, otherwise undated).
37. *J:* V, 353 (Aug. 7, 1853).
38. *W,* p. 312.
39. *J:* XIII, 20–21 (Dec. 12, 1859).
40. *J:* VI, 322 (June 1, 1854).
41. *VW,* p. 46.
42. *Ibid.,* p. 168.
43. *J:* III, 400 (Apr. 11, 1852).
44. *J:* XII, 170–71 (May 1, 1859).
45. *J:* XIV, 131 (Oct. 16, 1860).
46. *J:* V, 246 (June 13, 1853).
47. *J:* VIII, 220–21 (Mar. 23, 1856).
48. *MW,* p. 253.
49. *J:* I, 300 (Dec. 26, 1841).
50. *VW,* pp. 49–50.
51. *J:* VII, 53 (Sept. 24, 1854).
52. *J:* V, 265 (June 17, 1853).
53. *J:* VI, 21 (Dec. 18, 1853).
54. *E,* p. 13.
55. *J:* XII, 412 (Oct. 21, 1859).
56. *J:* XI, 451 (Feb. 16, 1859).
57. *J:* II, 434 (July 16, 1850).
58. *J:* V, 75 (Mar. 30, 1853).
59. *J:* III, 24 (Sept. 26, 1851).
60. *J:* I, 73 (Feb. 8, 1839).
61. *W,* pp. 101–2.

Chapter 5

1. *J:* V, 87 (Apr. 21, 1853).
2. *J:* VI, 200 (Apr. 16, 1854).
3. *J:* I, 36–40 (Mar. 14, 1838).
4. *Ibid.,* p. 37.
5. *Ibid.,* p. 40.
6. *W,* p. 133. The triple indictment in the citation applies only to the burden of a political state. However, the burden of society, which in this chapter includes both the society of friends and the society of countrymen, makes the phrase generally as well as particularly applicable. The point is the unnecessary burden, not the specific kind of burden.
7. *J:* IX, 479 (July 13, 1857).

8. *J:* III, 146 (Dec. 21, 1851).
9. *J:* I, 107 (Fall, 1839).
10. *J:* III, 304 (Feb. 14, 1852).
11. *J:* IX, 479 (July 14, 1857).
12. *J:* VIII, 230 (Mar. 28, 1856).
13. *W,* p. 305.
14. *J:* I, 107 (Fall, 1839).
15. *J:* IX, 216 (Jan. 11, 1857).
16. *J:* VIII, 348 (May 19, 1856).
17. *J:* V, 130 (May 8, 1853).
18. *J:* X, 146 (Oct. 29, 1857).
19. *J:* XI, 282 (Nov. 3, 1858).
20. *J:* I, 382 (Aug. 15, 1845).
21. *J:* I, 80 (June 22, 1839).
22. *J:* I, 204 (Feb. 7, 1841).
23. *J:* I, 290 (Nov. 30, 1841).
24. *J:* I, 107 (Fall, 1839).
25. *J:* I, 469 (1837–1847, otherwise undated).
26. *J:* I, 113 (Jan. 26, 1840).
27. *J:* I, 115 (Jan. 29, 1840).
28. *W,* p. 292.
29. *J:* I, 108 (Fall, 1839).
30. *J:* I, 438–40, 448 (1837–1847, otherwise undated).
31. *W,* p. 303.
32. *J:* III, 262 (Feb. 1, 1852).
33. *J:* V, 87 (Apr. 21, 1853).
34. *J:* II, 143 (Jan. 10, 1851).
35. *J:* V, 515 (Nov. 21, 1853).
36. *J:* III, 389–90 (Apr. 4, 1852).
37. *J:* V, 188 (May 24, 1853). This and the preceding citation refer to Thoreau's unstable friendship with Emerson.
38. *J:* II, 98 (Nov. 16, 1850).
39. *J:* III, 265 (Feb. 1, 1852).
40. *J:* VI, 200 (Apr. 16, 1854).
41. *J:* II, 161 (Feb. 15, 1851).
42. *J:* IX, 266–67, 277, 279 (Feb. 23–24, 1857).
43. *J:* IV, 46–47 (May 11, 1852).
44. *C,* p. 147 (to Helen Thoreau, Oct. 18, 1843). The reference is "to Channing and all that fraternity."
45. *J:* IV, 313–14 (Aug. 24, 1852).
46. *J:* IV, 262 (July 27, 1852).
47. *J:* III, 400 (Apr. 11, 1852).
48. *J:* VII, 416–17 (June 10, 1855).
49. *P,* p. 49.

50. *W*, p. 133.
51. *CC*, p. 368.
52. *Ibid.*, pp. 364–66.
53. *J:* VI, 355 (June 16, 1854). See also *J:* XII, 409 (Oct. 19, 1859).
54. *J:* VIII, 189 (Feb. 27, 1856).
55. *E*, p. 27.
56. *J:* XIV, 304 (Jan. 3, 1861).
57. *C*, p. 430 (to Bronson Alcott, Sept. 1, 1856).
58. *J:* VI, 358 (June 16, 1854).
59. *CC*, p. 374.
60. *Ibid.*, p. 376.
61. *Ibid.*
62. *Ibid.*, p. 382.
63. *J:* VII, 150 (Jan. 27, 1855).
64. *CC*, p. 389.
65. *J:* VI, 339 (June 9, 1854).
66. *CC*, pp. 416, 429.
67. *Ibid*, p. 408.
68. *VW*, p. 174.
69. *J:* XII, 430 (Oct. 22, 1859).
70. *CC*, p. 407.
71. *Ibid.*, p. 431.
72. *J:* XII, 401 (Oct. 19, 1859).
73. *CC*, p. 389.

Chapter 6

1. *J:* II, 440 (Sept. 1, 1851).
2. *J:* IX, 117 (Oct. 16, 1856).
3. *CC*, pp. 455–82. The essay was originally published, posthumously, in *The Atlantic Monthly*, Oct., 1863.
4. *Ibid.*, p. 463.
5. *Ibid.*, p. 482.
6. *J:* II, 101 (Nov. 16, 1850).
7. *J:* IV, 129 (June 22, 1852).
8. *C*, p. 221 (to H. G. O. Blake, May 2, 1848).
9. *J:* II, 76 (Oct. 31, 1850).
10. *J:* II, 277 (June 29, 1851).
11. *J:* I, 12 (Nov. 18, 1837).
12. *J:* X, 227 (Dec. 27, 1857).
13. *J:* X, 188 (Nov. 18, 1857).

14. *J:* I, 56 (Aug. 27, 1837).
15. *J:* I, 295 (Dec. 15, 1841).
16. *J:* I, 214 (Feb. 14, 1841).
17. *J:* V, 377 (Aug. 16, 1853).
18. *P,* p. 141.
19. *W,* p. 35.
20. *J:* XII, 420 (Feb. 3, 1859).
21. *CC,* p. 108.
22. *J:* X, 76 (Oct. 7, 1857).
23. *VW,* p. 136.
24. *J:* XII, 437 (Oct. 22, 1859).
25. *HS,* p. 19.
26. *C,* p. 641 (to Myron Benton, Mar. 21, 1862).
27. *HS,* pp. 310–11 (letter from Sophia Thoreau to Daniel Ricketson, dated May 20, 1862).
28. *J:* VI, 80 (Jan. 27, 1854).
29. *J:* X, 309 (Mar. 19, 1858).
30. *MW,* p. 77.
31. *Ibid.,* p. 71.
32. *C,* pp. 511–12 (to Marston Watson, Apr. 25, 1858).
33. *J:* II, 440 (Sept. 1, 1851).
34. *J:* II, 449 (Sept. 3, 1851).
35. *J:* X, 259 (Jan. 26, 1858).
36. *J:* IX, 117 (Oct. 16, 1856).
37. *J:* VII, 236 (Mar. 9, 1855).
38. *J:* VII, 527 (Oct. 29, 1855).
39. *J:* X, 114 (Oct. 21, 1857).
40. *J:* VII, 10 (Sept. 4, 1854).
41. *J:* VI, 98–99 (Feb. 5, 1854).
42. *J:* V, 242 (June 11, 1853).
43. *J:* XIII, 332 (June 6, 1860).
44. *J:* XIII, 243 (Apr. 6, 1860).
45. *J:* XII, 129–30 (Dec. 24, 1850).
46. *J:* III, 212 (Jan. 21, 1852).
47. *J:* VIII, 79 (Jan. 1, 1856).
48. *J:* IX, 16 (Aug. 23, 1856).
49. *J:* XIII, 345–46 (June 11, 1860).
50. *VW,* p. 255.
51. *W,* pp. 236–37.
52. *CC,* p. 163.
53. *Ibid.,* p. 124.
54. *Ibid.,* p. 8.
55. *Ibid.,* p. 11.
56. *C,* p. 62 (to Mrs. Lucy Brown, Mar. 2, 1842).

57. *J:* V, 283 (June 20, 1853).
58. *J:* IV, 149–50 (June 26, 1852).
59. *J:* X, 151 (Oct. 31, 1857).
60. *J:* VI, 162 (Mar. 10, 1854).
61. *J:* IX, 309–10 (Mar. 28, 1857).
62. *VW,* p. 183.
63. *J:* XIV, 158 (Oct. 20, 1860).
64. *J:* XIV, 268 (Nov. 25, 1860).
65. *E,* p. 270.
66. *W,* pp. 178–79.
67. *MW,* p. 200.
68. *J:* III, 366–67 (Mar. 31, 1852).
69. *J:* I, 217 (Feb. 19, 1841).
70. *C,* p. 64 (to Emerson, Mar. 11, 1842).
71. *CC,* p. 71.
72. *C,* p. 62 (to Mrs. Lucy Brown, Mar. 2, 1842).
73. *J:* XIV, 284 (Nov. 29, 1860).
74. *J:* I, 283 (Sept. 5, 1841).

Chapter 7

1. *J:* VII, 383 (May 23, 1855).
2. *J:* XIV, 117 (Oct. 13, 1860).
3. *E,* pp. 249–89. The essay was originally published, posthumously, in *The Atlantic Monthly,* Oct., 1862.
4. *Ibid.,* pp. 262–63.
5. *Ibid.,* p. 264.
6. *Ibid.,* pp. 288–89.
7. *J:* IX, 223 (Jan. 15, 1857).
8. *J:* III, 95 (Nov. 7, 1851).
9. *J:* XIV, 274 (Nov. 26, 1860).
10. *J:* VIII, 88–89 (Jan. 5, 1856).
11. *J:* II, 15 (May 12, 1850).
12. *J:* VIII, 14 (Nov. 7, 1855).
13. *J:* VIII, 18 (Nov. 9, 1855).
14. *J:* II, 428 (Aug. 28, 1851).
15. *J:* X, 53–54 (Sept. 30, 1857).
16. *J:* IX, 337 (Apr. 23, 1857).
17. *J:* VIII, 19 (Nov. 9, 1855).
18. *J:* XIII, 160 (Feb. 23, 1860).
19. *J:* X, 164–65 (Nov. 5, 1857).
20. *J:* V, 45 (Mar. 23, 1853).

21. *J:* IV, 174 (July 2, 1852).
22. *J:* IV, 351 (Sept. 13, 1852).
23. *J:* IV, 9 (May 2, 1852).
24. *MW,* p. 135.
25. *J:* VI, 253 (May 10, 1854).
26. *J:* IV, 31 (May 7, 1852).
27. *W,* p. 388.
28. *J:* XIII, 195 (Mar. 15, 1860).
29. *J:* V, 139 (May 10, 1853).
30. *J:* XIV, 117 (Oct. 13, 1860).
31. *J:* XII, 23 (Mar. 7, 1859).
32. *J:* IV, 163 (June 29, 1852).
33. *J:* XII, 343 (Sept. 23, 1859).
34. *J:* XII, 389 (Oct. 16, 1859).
35. *J:* VI, 85 (Jan. 30, 1854).
36. *CC,* p. 3.
37. *W,* p. 36.
38. *J:* V, 472 (Nov. 2, 1853).
39. *J:* IV, 80 (June 4, 1852).
40. *E,* pp. 285–86.
41. *J:* II, 193 (May 6, 1851).
42. *W,* p. 330.
43. *J:* IV, 126 (June 21, 1852).
44. *J:* XIII, 77 (Jan. 4, 1860).
45. *J:* XI, 285 (Nov. 4, 1858).
46. *J:* V, 323 (July 21, 1853).
47. *J:* VIII, 44 (Dec. 11, 1855).
48. *J:* XIV, 306 (Jan. 3, 1861).
49. *W,* p. 405.
50. *J:* X, 252 (Jan. 23, 1858).
51. *J:* XIII, 311 (May 24, 1860).
52. *J:* IV, 190 (July 5, 1852).
53. *J:* V, 292 (June 22, 1853).
54. *J:* V, 158 (May 15, 1853).
55. *MW,* p. 41.
56. *VW,* p. 115.
57. *J:* XIV, 174–75 (Oct. 25, 1860).
58. *J:* I, 77 (Apr. 9, 1839).
59. *J:* XI, 206 (Oct. 12, 1858).
60. *VW,* p. 249.
61. *J:* VIII, 222–23 (Mar. 23, 1856).
62. *J:* IX, 209 (Jan. 7, 1857).
63. *J:* I, 131 (Mar. 22, 1840).
64. *J:* IX, 32 (Aug. 28, 1856).

65. *J:* VI, 474 (Aug. 26, 1854).
66. *W,* p. 11.
67. *J:* X, 299 (Mar. 16, 1858).
68. *J:* VI, 131–32 (Feb. 19, 1854).
69. *J:* XI, 204 (Oct. 10, 1858).
70. *J:* III, 165 (Dec. 30, 1851).
71. *J:* VIII, 110 (Jan. 13, 1856).
72. *J:* VIII, 43 (Dec. 11, 1855).
73. *E,* p. 125.
74. *W,* p. 34.
75. *J:* XIV, 166 (Oct. 22, 1860).
76. Thoreau as quoted in M. D. Conway: *Autobiography* (Boston, 1904), I, 148.

Chapter 8

1. *J:* II, 424–25 (July 16, 1850).
2. *J:* II, 162 (Feb. 16, 1851).
3. *CC,* p. 611 ff.
4. *J:* II, 274 (June 29, 1851).
5. *W,* p. 7.
6. Letter to Orestes Brownson, dated Oct. 29, 1854. The manuscript is owned by the University of Notre Dame.
7. *J:* II, 22–24 (late May, 1850).
8. *J:* I, 61 (Dec. 7, 1838).
9. *J:* I, 362–63 (July 6, 1845).
10. *CC,* p. 396.
11. *J:* XII, 420 (Oct. 22, 1859).
12. *CC,* p. 443.
13. *J:* VI, 313–15 (May 29, 1854).
14. *CC,* p. 313.
15. *J:* II, 162 (Feb. 16, 1851).
16. *J:* XIV, 292 (Dec. 4, 1860).
17. *C,* p. 20 (to Orestes Brownson, Dec. 30, 1837).
18. *J:* II, 83 (Oct., 1850).
19. *J:* II, 141 (Jan. 10, 1851).
20. *J:* V, 459–60 (Oct. 27, 1853).
21. *J:* III, 196 (Jan. 16, 1852).
22. *J:* I, 227 (Mar. 3, 1841).
23. *J:* VII, 503 (Oct. 20, 1855).
24. *VW,* p. 26.
25. *J:* XIV, 260 (Nov. 22, 1860).

26. *J:* I, 367–68 (July 14, 1845).
27. *J:* II, 403 (Aug. 19, 1851).
28. *J:* VII, 167–68 (Feb. 3, 1855).
29. *J:* VII, 268–69 (Mar. 24, 1855).
30. *J:* VIII, 454 (Aug. 8, 1856).
31. *E,* pp. 240–41.
32. *P,* p. 206.
33. *J:* V, 410–12 (Sept. 1, 1853).
34. *J:* IX, 160 (Dec. 5, 1856).
35. *J:* XII, 297 (Aug. 27, 1859).
36. *J:* IX, 246 (Feb. 8, 1857).
37. *HS,* p. 150.
38. *C,* p. 224 (to Horace Greeley, May 19, 1848).
39. *J:* I, 134 (Apr. 22, 1840).
40. *VW,* p. 40.
41. *Ibid.,* p. 263.
42. *J:* IX, 350 (May 1, 1857).
43. *VW,* p. 71.
44. *J:* VIII, 8 (Nov. 5, 1855).
45. *J:* IV, 198 (July 7, 1852).
46. *J:* V, 424 (Sept. 12, 1853).
47. *J:* V, 445 (Oct. 22, 1853).
48. *HS,* p. 153.
49. *P,* p. 3.
50. *J:* VII, 51 (Sept. 22, 1854).
51. *J:* V, 34 (Mar. 21, 1853).
52. *C,* p. 40 (to Helen Thoreau, June 13, 1840).
53. *VW,* p. 136.
54. *J:* VIII, 204 (Mar. 11, 1856).
55. *J:* III, 85 (Nov. 1, 1851).
56. *VW,* p. 104.
57. *J:* II, 44–45 (July 16, 1850).
58. *J:* XI, 89 (Aug. 9, 1858).
59. *J:* I, 407–8 (1845–1847, otherwise undated).
60. *J:* V, 19 (Mar. 12, 1853).

Chapter 9

1. *J:* XI, 112–13 (Aug. 18, 1858).
2. *W,* p. 129.
3. *J:* I, 280 (Sept. 2, 1841).
4. *The Dial* (Jan., 1843), III, 331–40.

5. *Ibid.*, p. 340.
6. *VW*, p. 125.
7. *C*, p. 284 (to Sophia Thoreau, July 13, 1852).
8. *CC*, p. 469.
9. *VW*, p. 69.
10. *W*, p. 67.
11. *J:* II, 3 (early May, 1850).
12. *W*, pp. 72–73.
13. *Ibid.*, p. 74.
14. *Ibid.*
15. *C*, p. 579 (to H. G. O. Blake, May 20, 1860).
16. *W*, p. 79.
17. *J:* X, 289–90 (Mar. 2, 1858).
18. *J:* IX, 344 (Apr. 26, 1857).
19. *J:* XII, 247 (July 20, 1859).
20. *E*, pp. 161–62.
21. *VW*, p. 185.
22. *HS*, p. 28.
23. *J:* I, 452 (Oct. 21, 1842).
24. *J:* V, 293 (June 22, 1853).
25. *J:* I, 308 (Jan. 1, 1842).
26. *J:* I, 359 (Apr. 3, 1842).
27. *J:* I, 316 (Jan. 8, 1842).
28. *J:* I, 265 (Aug. 1, 1841).
29. *J:* I, 140 (June 15, 1840).
30. *VW*, p. 88.
31. *Ibid.*, p. 261.
32. *Ibid.*, p. 30.
33. *P*, p. 42.
34. *VW*, p. 258.
35. *Ibid.*, p. 256.
36. *J:* VI, 352–53 (June 16, 1854).
37. *J:* VI, 336 (June 8, 1854).
38. *VW*, p. 80.
39. *Ibid.*, p. 29.
40. *J:* V, 275 (June 18, 1853).
41. *VW*, pp. 121–22.
42. *J:* VI, 426 (Aug. 7, 1854).
43. *VW*, p. 184.
44. *J:* I, 326 (Mar. 11, 1842).
45. *J:* III, 179 (Jan. 8, 1852).
46. *J:* VIII, 113 (Jan. 12, 1855).
47. *VW*, p. 89.
48. *Ibid.*, p. 93.

49. *P*, p. 230.
50. *J:* VI, 4 (Dec. 2, 1853).
51. *W*, p. 182.
52. *CC*, p. 13.
53. *W*, p. 129.
54. *VW*, pp. 261–63.
55. *J:* I, 18 (Dec. 17, 1837).
56. *J:* XI, 112–13 (Aug. 18, 1858).
57. *J:* I, 64–69 (Dec. 15, 1838).
58. *W*, p. 418.

Afterword

1. *J:* I, 350 (Mar. 26, 1842).
2. *J:* I, 351–52 (Mar. 27, 1842).
3. *J:* I, 300 (Dec. 26, 1841).

INDEX

Acceptance, 43, 44
Action, deliberateness of, 39-40;
 not a measure of a man, 22
Adam, 122-123, 132
Aestheticism, 31, 34
Alcott, Bronson, 8, 73
America, call for revolt against
 government, 82; natural re-
 sources of, 102; plea to dis-
 cover rural, 36; view of
 American states, 80, 81-82
Apple tree, 54ff.
Association for the Advancement
 of Science, 31
"Autumnal Tints," 102

Balzac, Honoré de, 109
Baskin, Leonard, 150
Beauty, in nature, 110, 111, 115;
 perception of as a moral test,
 111
Bhagavad Gita, 134
Bible, *Book of Joel,* 56-57; *Co-
 rinthians,* 13, 16; "lilies-of-the-
 field" parable, 128; New Testa-
 ment, 138-139; references to,
 16, 20, 133
Body, physical condition of, 89;
 and the self, 29, 31; and the
 soul, 29, 132; vigor of, 41, 47
Bonhoeffer, Dietrich, 133
Brahma, 28, 134, 136, 147
Bravery, 4, 41
Brown, John, 92, 123
"Brute Neighbors," 102
Business (See Commerce)

Calvinism, 134
Camoens, Luiz Vaz de, 117
Cape Cod, 102
Channing, Ellery, 8, 44
Character, genius and, 8-9; and
 independence of the self, 27;
 as measure of a man, 22

Chaucer, Geoffrey, 145
Christ, Jesus, 136
Christianity, Thoreau's ambivalence toward, 138; in Concord,
 139-141; Thoreau's interest in,
 61, 75, 133
Cities, 59-60, 66
"Civil Disobedience," 7, 124
Civilization, customs and conventions, 61; and the "dead unkind," 65, 66, 67; and defile-
 ment of nature, 64ff.; as de-
 filer of life, 56; as hindrance to
 purpose, 43; and mass living, 60
Clothing, 128
Coleridge, Samuel Taylor, 106
Commerce, commercial slaves,
 125-126; commercial spirit, 125;
 immorality of, 84, 85; inter-
 ference with life, 85
Complexity (See Simplicity)
Concord, farming in, 63-64; reli-
 gion in, 134, 137, 139-140, 146;
 Thoreau in, 6, 63, 102; Tran-
 scendentalism in, 12
Conduct of life, 14, 15, 84, 135-
 136, 140
Confucianism, 138
Connections, 125
Conscience, 142, 154
"Conscious" (See Soul)
Consciousness, 30, 151ff.
Conventions, 61
Conviction, 48
Criticism by Thoreau, of Sir
 Walter Raleigh, 22; of those
 who seek wealth, 25
Crowds, 59, 60, 66
Custom, 61

"Dead unkind," 65, 66, 67
Death, 90-91, 97, 113, 129
Decay in nature, 115
Deliberateness, 39-40, 49

[173]